In
Search
of God

W. Herbstrith

In Search of God

Meditation in the Christian Tradition

New City Press

Published in the United States by New City Press
202 Cardinal Rd., Hyde Park, NY 12538
©1989 New City Press

Translated by Edward Flood and Gary Brandl
from the original German edition *Verweilen vor Gott*
©1977 Verlag Herder, Freiburg, Germany

Cover art by Nick Cianfarani

Library of Congress Cataloging-in-Publication Data:

Herbstrith, Waltraud.
    [Verweilen vor Gott. English]
    In search of God / W. Herbstrith ; [translated by Edward Flood and
Gary Brandl from the original German edition].
    ISBN 1-56548-067-8 : $7.95

    1. Meditation–Catholic Church.   2. Catholic Church—Doctrines.
    3. Teresa, of Avila, Saint, 1515-1582.   4. John of the Cross, Saint,
1542-1591.   5. Thérèse, de Lisieux, Saint, 1873-1897.   6. Stein,
Edith, 1891-1942.   7. Carmelites—Spiritual life.   8. Carmelite
Nuns—Spiritual life.   I. Title
    BX2350.2.H39   1994
    248.3'4–dc20   94-10244

1st printing: April 1989
3d printing (new ed.): April 1994

Scriptural quotations are from *The New American Bible*
©1970 Confraternity of Christian Doctrine

Printed in the United States of America

CONTENT

PREFACE

Even though modern technology has provided life with many comforts and new conveniences, people today are searching earnestly for the meaning of life, for someone who can shed light on its mysteries and hardships. The present day attention given to Oriental meditation and philosophies, in the hope of finding meaningful answers to the questions posed in modern society, is only one of the many indications of this search.

It is very worthwhile to pursue these points of contact with the Orient, however they should also serve to help us rediscover the heredity of the West, and better appreciate its religious and cultural values.

The following chapters present ideas that stem from a tradition of Christian meditation. The contemplative Carmelite order takes its name from Mount Carmel, in Israel, from where it traces its origins. Teresa of Avila, John of the Cross, Thérèse of Lisieux and Edith Stein belonged to this order. Notwithstanding their diverse nationalities and upbringing, they were all spiritual inhabitants of Carmel. They understood the necessity of meditating upon the profound and transforming mystery of Christ and lived for this ideal.

People today are in greater need of practices and guidelines for managing their lives. God must not become just a number nor remain an unknown territory. People today need to learn again how to pause for a moment to stand before him. These four personalities of the Carmel can become expert companions for life's journey to reach God. The helps proposed for learning to appreciate the value of meditation do not come from the mere desire to formulate theories. This book is an attempt to honor the many requests made to the Author to describe what meditation actually means.

Waltraud Herbstrith

PART ONE

RELIGIOUS LIFE
IN THE MIDST OF THE WORLD

I. INTRODUCTION

For the Christian, to live in a contemplative fashion or, as it is said nowadays, as a meditative individual totally immersed in the human reality, does not imply a static contemplation of a divinity or an eternal treasure, but establishing a personal relationship with someone called Jesus Christ. Consequently, in order to be true Christians our personal relationships must always be oriented toward Christ.

According to the same static understanding, the notion of a contemplative vocation has often been contrasted to "external" activity. Contemplative life, especially that of a cloister, has been rigidly differentiated from the so-called active life. In this regard, we have been drawn more than once to the passage referring to Mary and Martha in the Gospel of Saint Luke (cf. 10:38-42), in which Jesus praises Mary and reproves Martha. Thomas Aquinas, Master Eckhart, Teresa of Avila[1] and other authors did not share this exegesis, since they consider that the perfect Christian life is fulfilled in a harmonious unity between prayer and action. It should also be remembered that Greek writers on asceticism such as Evagrius and Maximus the Confessor, use terms such as "active life" and "contemplative life," and with "active life" are not referring to a life of immediate service such as preaching, teaching, social work, or something similar, but to the inner struggle required to defeat one's passions and acquire the virtues. This is as much the task of the so-called contemplative orders—communities where inner prayer and meditation occupy a privileged place—as it is of every working man and woman.[2]

Nowadays, we often ask ourselves what is it that helps us to be responsible and committed Christians. The answer lies in our orientation towards the person of Jesus Christ, and in allowing his Holy Spirit to penetrate our lives. It often happens that people acting purely human are more Christ-like than others who affirm to be Christian. God can be close to us in all the ways of thinking of our times; it is up to us to pause and examine their closeness or distance to the message of Christ.

The question about whether Christianity must always consciously inform all aspects of life should be formulated more radically: Shouldn't Jesus be, for Christians, the Lord that informs everything?

Our present times suffer the disease of poor human relationships and an overemphasis on efficiency. We are expected to act in a practical and efficient way. If this demand dominates our personal needs and makes us incapable of thinking in terms of personal values, it alters our being human.

Our conscience has been changed. It is said today that there are new ways of understanding. We can no longer talk about God in the ingenuous way previous generations have done. Faced by the challenge of atheism—whose arguments are many times our own—we are often invaded by what Thérèse of Lisieux experienced at the end of her short life:

the sensation that God had abandoned her, spiritual tediousness, inner darkness. However, by overstressing the so-called "absence of God" our disbelief could even become appealing to us. Moreover, we fear the effort it takes to become aware of God's closeness. In fact, even in times of inner darkness and need, God can manifest himself to the person who listens, yearns, and prays.

The followers of Christ can start their apostolic work only when it is evident that what sustains them is a personal encounter with God. To what else could they otherwise testify by their actions? We Christians are often surpassed by non-Christians when it comes to loving, being tolerant, and finding solutions for life's problems. Schillebeeckx says that the nonbeliever also lives in God without knowing it, and without following any given religion.[3]

It often happened that greater consideration was given to prayer than to work, and it was believed that work needed to be transformed into "prayer." However, today we go to the opposite extreme by believing that in order to be Christians it is enough to be humble and work conscientiously; thus implying that prayer is a loss of time or a type of daydreaming. We don't realize that times of rest are becoming ever more important to us.

Work and prayer do go together, yet each one is also essential in itself. Nowadays, people talk about a "rehabilitation of matter" (Krasinsky); in the same way, we could talk of a rehabilitation of work.

To pray means to respond to a call that is made to us; this requires our being silent in order to hear it. Praying may mean to speak, to contemplate, to stay still without talking, or to abandon ourselves. Work is something that can be done in the presence of God through an attitude of giving and loving. It should be done in total freedom—of which we become particularly aware in prayer—not enslaved in a senseless order of the world.

The goal of unifying work and prayer, meditation and apostolate, can only be reached if we learn to make our actions spring forth from a personal center. This can happen through our exercise of prayer and in performing our work well. We may not always be able to think about God or pray while at work, but in every material aspect and detail of our work we can still direct our actions devotedly to God.

As far as our training in prayer is concerned, there is an important point to be mentioned. Our referring to God as someone whom we can turn to, and to Jesus as a person who is before us, is not enough to make our actions completely personal. A bond between perception and action will hardly be possible if certain psychological principles are not taken into account. We cannot deal into depth with two persons at the same time, otherwise—psychologically speaking—we shall neglect either our neighbor or God. In order to have a true, personal love for our neighbor, we should be able to spend more time with God in silence, allowing ourselves a special time in which we willingly decide to be alone with Him.

It is considered natural that friends should find some time to dedicate to each other outside their work environment. Without this "time for the other," the encounter with our neighbor—and similarly, the encounter with God—would become dry. If we consider it impossible to find God in our silent and personal meditation, neither shall we find him in our neighbor. Such a God would be a ghost. The only God that exists is the one I find also in silence, as a result of my free and personal search.

The linkage between prayer and work, between meditation and apostolate, requires a personal union with Jesus Christ. Any theological research that does not pay attention to what the Holy Spirit tells us, would be only tedious speculation. A liturgical celebration that does not pause in silence before God, would be a show. A job whose end does not benefit others would be pointless. In everything we do, we should be interiorly touched and transformed by the Spirit of Jesus.

II. WHAT IS MEDITATION?

1. The Fundamental Problem

From the question this chapter heading raises, we deduce that nowadays, a time in which there is such a great need for spirituality, the word meditation can have different meanings. Undoubtedly, its concept is not clear to everyone; in fact, it is a word that disorients some people. Many believe that meditation competes with authentic Christian prayer, ignoring the fact that it is not possible to pray in a Christian manner without meditating.

Still, we had better not anticipate the conclusions but rather raise first the question: what would our human existence be like without meditation? From this we can indirectly learn the meaning of meditation in its deepest sense, without implying, however, that with this we know everything about meditation.

What would our daily life be like without meditation? It would be similar to a cut flower which, even if purposely placed in a vase filled with water, can only keep fresh for a short length of time. What would the affection between a man and a woman be like without meditation? It would be incapable of establishing a lasting life together, of leaving space for faithfulness, for devotion, for working out difficult situations. What would friendship be like without meditation? Mutual exploitation, the enrichment of one person at the expense of the other. It would be like being deaf to one's fellow human beings, intolerant of their frustrations, and not allowing them to be themselves.

What would science be like without meditation? Pure rational thinking, torn away from the depth of consciousness, incapable of leading humankind to greater depth and maturity. What would technology be like without meditation? The manipulation of the human being through the inventions of his own mind, the inability to control machines and rockets and prevent deadly hazards. What would our Christian life be like without meditation? A mechanical repetition of prayers, the compliance with moral regulations and forms that prevent humankind from being free, and instead make it lazy, awkward, and atrophied; in short, a scandal for the non-believers. What would life without meditation be for those men and women who for love of their faith renounced matrimony in order to bear witness to the fact that the invisible reality of God is greater than the visible horizon of the earth? It would be like being faithful to an alien regulation, renouncing precious earthly goods, without rendering other deeper values visible and tangible.

From these questions we can draw some precious indications as to the behavior of the individual who meditates. Let us examine the most important ones. Meditation has something to do with establishing oneself, with persevering, with allowing space for and being certain about something or someone. In the process of meditating we let the persons we meet be themselves, we listen to them and become capable of recognizing them as individuals different from us, each of whom we address as another "you." From a life lived only within a rational structure, we enter the depths of our being, thus becoming more open and more mature. We learn to deal with our fellow human beings and daily circumstances with greater reflection and we act in a more reasonable and personal way. By meditating we learn, together with Saint Paul, that we are called to be free, unbound to false constraints. Even non-believers may find in meditation something that transcends their human limitations. The more we as Christians believe and depend on meditation, the more aware we shall become of a transcendence that will help us draw ourselves away from short-lived, temporal things. This transcendental being will become as a father and a mother to us. "As a mother comforts her son, so will I comfort you," Isaiah (66:13) wrote more than seven hundred years before Christ. And Jesus, in whom God's Revelation to humankind has been fulfilled, refers to God not as to a judge or illustrious lord, but calls him "kind-hearted father," "Abba—Dad."

Therefore, when we meditate, our every action and operation adopts a deep-rooted behavior that proceeds from a deeper level of ourselves and makes our lives ever more meaningful. Unfortunately, we often neglect this dimension and we hide and smother it, thus risking to become slaves of superficiality.

The simple and heated question is how to acquire the courage to become someone who meditates. Where should we turn for help? There can only be one answer: it is necessary to *start* meditating. Only when I begin to engage in this exercise, do I start to experience freedom from myself. At this point, though, fear may assail us: don't we already live our entire day under stress? Don't we look forward to our spare time during the weekend, to being free at last from all our burdens? Having to meditate sounds like additional work, like extra effort to exert.

Still, why should we expect things to be different for us, than what they were for Teresa of Avila and John of the Cross, who have been proclaimed Doctors of the Church? Both of them experienced the fear of silence and the tediousness of their exercises, and Teresa even more than John. Still, they recognized and announced, not only to some of their contemporaries but to the whole Church, that to meditate is to spend time with God deep inside our hearts. It means being with someone who loves us more than does any other human being. And this should neither imply stress nor work, but only joy, inner dialogue, relaxation from useless worries, and the experience of being close to God's mercy. Both these Doctors of the Church—and not only they, but the tradition of prayer as a whole—have demonstrated that we cannot be aware of God's love unless we are ready to silence our hearts for a while, to thank him for the fact that he exists and that he has allowed us to stay close to him.

We often hear complaints about the confusion that reigns in our present time, and the ugly world in which we live, about the declining number of churchgoers, and the antireligious attitude of the young people. These pessimistic voices do not entirely correspond to reality. In fact, it would also be reasonable to say that the resulting manipulation and collectivism in human society, the misuse of technology, the isolation and sense of danger, awaken in us the need to be silent, to feel accepted, to understand the meaning of things. Above all, the young are showing signs of a promising turning point towards authenticity and depth. A parish minister once told me: "During the celebration of the Eucharist, after proclaiming God's word or after receiving Holy Communion, I find it difficult to insert pauses for silence that can provide the faithful a chance to think about the word announced to them or about who they have just received. The primitive form of the divine service, as an unchangeable rhythm of prayer, which took very little account of silence as an opportunity for personal reflection, often prevented the believers to accept a new form. In contrast, some of the young people who feel the need for silence during the liturgy urged me to look into this because they wanted to organize a special mass to meet this need." Some worried Christian parents confess that their teenage children run after gurus and Oriental masters, and have lost interest in the Church.

At this point we ask ourselves why so many young people no longer experience the joy of attending mass. Perhaps it is because we have not paid enough attention to their need for meditation and have offered them a religion that no longer satisfies them. While the Oriental spiritual masters meet their demands for silence and self-search, and their need to be accepted, Christian environments often neglect these elements essential to every human being.

How little enticing some statements such as this sound: "The time dedicated to prayer should not be too long. I'm a hard worker and if I am to attend mass, I don't need a long service with too many silent pauses." I ask myself what is it we wish to find in mass. Perhaps a religious practice to prove to ourselves that we are devout? Shouldn't we rather listen to its call that urges us to undergo a transformation and allow the religious event to become a part of our lives? If the young generation is no longer satisfied with religious practices that provide little opportunity for their personal fulfillment, this should be seen as something positive rather than negative.

Let us think of the Taizé phenomenon. Whoever visits Taizé, the small locality in Burgundy, France, homeland of Saint Bernard of Clairvaux, is struck by the atmosphere of holiness and prayer and the fervent preaching of the monks. The latter have undertaken the monastic life—which represents a rediscovery of monasticism at the heart of Protestantism—in order to honor God, disregarding the fame they may have gained in the world. Still, the ways of the Lord are unpredictable. In thirty years, their community and secluded life have become a sign of Christian unity and love visible from afar.

This is the amazing point: young people of different religious creeds meet at Taizé to pray. And the prayers they use are not only those compiled according to liturgical standards, which the monks recite many times during the day as in every monastic community, but are above all silent prayers, delivered with simplicity before God. When the small Romanesque church was no longer large enough for the flow of visitors, the Church of the Reconciliation was built, which later had to be enlarged, further still, with a tent. Those who ask in what manner people pray in this church outside the official praying hours, hear the unanimous answer: in silence. The youth use posters to indicate an area in the church reserved for silent prayer which everyone should respect. We ask how this silence is achieved and we are told that the church is open day and night. Each one behaves as better suits his or her prayer: sitting, kneeling, or lying on the ground. The only convention that is maintained, without any constraint or useless formula, is that of staying in silence before God.

2. Key Elements For Meditation

Three elements are essential to meditation:
a) a space of time set aside for the exercise;
b) silence;
c) turning to God as to another person.

a) A space of time set aside for the exercise

After joining the Carmelite order, Edith Stein found two daily hours for meditation, which was something that had been lacking in her life before then. She writes in a letter: "I love the divine office and I am displeased whenever I miss the choral prayer, even that of the little Hours [Matins and Vespers], but the foundations of our life are the two hours of meditation we have in our daily agenda. Only now that I enjoy this benefit do I know how much I was missing outside the convent."[1]

Still, this benefit cannot be exclusive of those who live in a monastery. Many people recognize today that, while living a life that has nothing to do with that of a cloister, meditation is an urgent need to which they must regularly dedicate a space of time. Among them are people of varied occupations, the young and the elderly. Already in the sixteenth century, Teresa of Avila believed that the personal relationship established with God deep inside our hearts—by meditation she meant inner prayer, the prayer of recollection, self-examination—was not reserved exclusively to those who live in a monastery. She tried to convert spouses, theologians, and business-people alike to the cause of meditation, so convinced was she that no human existence can do without the strength provided by meditation, reflection, and interior recollection.

The problem has always been and still is, especially today, how to find the time needed for recollection. Even though we acknowledge its value, meditation is often a difficult task; so we tend to fall into the opposite position and think that as a mother who is dedicated to her children or as a father who sacrifices himself to provide for his family, we already do enough. On top of this to add a period of time for meditation to our daily agenda would be a luxury, something for experts in spirituality, for priests and for those who belong to religious orders. This notion has never been and is not correct even today. In fact, even the mother who looks after her children, even those who have a job and have to keep in mind the responsibilities of their position, need some time for total solitude. Orthodox Metropolitan Anthony Bloom, who lives in London, used to tell about his father who, at a fixed time every day, would hang on the door of his room a piece of paper on which was written: "Even if I am in, I do not want to speak to anyone or answer the telephone for half an hour." This half-hour of silence and recollection offered him a pause that he considered absolutely necessary if he was to remain man and Christian in spite of the burden of his work and family preoccupations.

The fact that we require certain exercises to penetrate the depth of our hearts and knowledge of ourselves, belongs to our existence as human beings. Otherwise, we are not capable of going beyond the external bark of busy, absent-minded, perhaps even good workers, but who are not very attentive to their neighbor. We shall have no meaning for others if we are only halfway individuals, if we always lack the courage to be ourselves before ourselves and before God, through keeping silence. Why are we afraid to be silent? Why do we keep saying that we do not have an available half-hour for silence, while we spend so much time chatting or just idling about? It is part of our formation as individuals to dedicate some time to important personal activities. In fact, we have breakfast every morning at the same time. We usually stick to the same timetable for our lunch and an afternoon break. In the evening, we like to meet again and spend some time with our family and friends. Surely, what determines these daily pauses is not the food or the refreshment we take, but rather the longing to be with those who love us, to share with them a word, an experience, a preoccupation. The individual as a whole is interested in these pauses.

The same thing happens in relation to meditation, in spending some time before God, in listening to him. First of all, to pray does not mean merely to say something to God, to recite beautiful words, or to sing in church with other people for an hour every Sunday. To pray means to reawaken in ourselves the longing to be with God as with a human being, since God has become man in Christ Jesus. God has shown us that he loves us. We should pray not only when we feel it is spontaneous or when we are in the mood to do so. A woman once said to me: "I cannot say the Our Father every day; I often have no inclination to prayer at all. I'm able to say the Our Father only when I really feel touched by God." It is certainly beautiful to recite Jesus' prayer with our intimate participation. However, if we are always going to wait until God moves us before we pray, we may not do it for a long time and we will eventually become totally alien to our faith.

Therefore, it is important to establish a given time of the day for meditation—and each of us must discover what that best time is, in order not to depend on how we feel about it. In this way we can say to God: "This half-hour is for you, even though I don't have anything grandiose or wise to say to you. My only wish is to be with you and thank you, with my attention and my life, for being here."

If we acquire the habit of spending these periods of time patiently, even if we do not experience deep emotions, it can be very fruitful to our faith. We do not always experience the same feelings towards our best friends; still, we show them our love and understanding on a daily basis. There is a passage in the story of *The Little Prince* by Antoine de Saint-Exupéry in which the fox says to the little prince who pays it an unexpected visit: "It would have been better if you had returned at the usual time. In fact, if you come every day at four o'clock, I shall start to be glad at three o'clock. As the hour goes by, my gladness shall grow. By four o'clock I shall start to stir and be anxious; then I shall discover the price of happiness! But if I never know exactly what time you are coming, I shall not know when to prepare my heart for you.... Some things require rites!"[2]

b) Silence

We often hear the question: "Why does everything have to be so silent during meditation? God created us as beings who can communicate through the use of words. Isn't it then better to sing, individually or in chorus, to read a book, or even to look at a painting? What is the meaning of sitting there completely still, with our eyes closed? Isn't that perhaps something that has to do with the Far East, or something that, in any case, is foreign to Christianity?" The truth is we do not need to look to the East in order to rediscover the value of silence for our prayer and for our lives as human beings. The great Christian mystics and saints of the West teach unanimously: "The Lord himself will fight for you; you have only to keep still" (Ex 14:14).

Let us recall the prophets who prayed in the solitude of the desert before preaching to the people. Let us think of the great patriarchs of the Jewish people, of Abraham, Jacob, Moses, who, by keeping silent, held a fervent dialogue with God. Even when Jesus travelled across Israel he did not only preach and perform good works. His disciples noticed that he often retreated into solitude and silence, in order to pray better. This behavior of Jesus was surprising, particularly if we think that, except for a brief period of time, he did not live in the desert like John the Baptist or the community of Qumran. Jesus was not a monk, he lived among the common people; still, he always pursued silence and solitude with God.

Why is silence so important? Because it is like sowing a field that is ready to receive the seeds. How could the seed possibly grow if it does not find a suitable ground in which to live and develop! The ability to attain inner silence, to set aside those thoughts and images that are linked to our daily life, provide us with the right attitude we must keep in regards to people and things. We learn that we cannot dispose of anyone or anything; that every thing, every human being, has its own individuality, its right to exist, which we must treat respectfully. By being interiorly silent and empty, we experience that prayer is something different from what we commonly think. To pray means not so much to recite a prepared text, but rather to have the courage to engage in conversation with Jesus Christ in a completely personal manner. Whoever prays must learn to speak, as a child must do, by assimilating the words of the scriptures and the prayers of the saints.

But even the words of scripture or the prayers of others can become an obstacle for whoever prays if, at least from time to time, one does not have the courage to be silent and practice this radically. Like Adam, who did not want himself to be seen by God, we are capable of hiding even behind the holiest of words. We often fear God, even though we may not like to admit it. We believe he would reproach us and display our errors before us. The truth is exactly the opposite. The more relaxed and silent we become before God, the more honest we are in front of him; the more quiet—and let's be straightforward, the happier—we become. Some Christians believe that as long as you are a believer, you cannot be happy. They believe that things such as our responsibilities, the suffering of the world and Christ's cross are incompatible with our personal happiness. Yet, most saintly men, women, and people filled with God radiate joy among those who surround them. The Christian message does not refer to the suffering that characterizes the earthly lives, but rather to the joy in God, which surpasses every suffering, and to the Resurrection of the flesh in Jesus Christ. Even if during their life people have to undergo a lot of suffering, the proof of their being truly Christian is their joy, the joy of being called to exist, of being able to breathe and to live, of contributing to the development of the world, of being redeemed from sin. Suffering, injustice, and misery do not have to make us bitter nor pessimistic; on the contrary, our task is to contribute to transform the physical and spiritual suffering of our fellow human beings into the hope of a peaceful eternal life. This is not just a consolation found in the hope of a heavenly life. It is the truth about Jesus Christ and his message about God. This fullness of joy is given to us when, in being externally and interiorly silent, we think about God's love and say to him: "I am happy to be a creature of yours, I thank you for my being alive."

Silence has something in common with knowing how to wait, and waiting, with wanting to be and being at the disposal of our neighbor. There is a time when a barren field which has been sown prepares itself to produce grains and fruits, but it does not do this throughout the whole year. That is why to be barren is as important as to bear fruit and to give of our strength. If we always fail to be silent and empty before God like a field that waits patiently, we shall never bear fruit—or the fruits we bear shall be insignificant or diseased. Meditation is this emptiness, this silent emptiness, this waiting before God in order that he may enter our lives.

c) Turning to God as to another person

In dealing with the elements of meditation examined thus far—selecting a fixed time for our meditation, and the exercise to be done in silence—we have used the word "God" or "You." It should be obvious to the Christian that his or her meditation, his or her becoming interiorly free from the numerous thoughts and images produced in daily life, will not end in an emptiness experienced as a vague nothingness. "I know him in whom I have believed," Saint Paul says (2 Tm 1:12). The joy experienced by the believer in Christ, lies precisely on being able to say "you" to God, as to a human person. The silence of creation, the silence of two people that are close to each other, is not a silence that brings fear, or that makes us feel uncomfortable. Our faith tells us that we are loved and we believe that our earthly experience of love links us to the experience of God's love, which unifies and transcends everything. However, since God is an infinite mystery, since he creates our human condition and at the same time transcends it, we cannot simply compare the "you" we use in talking to our fellow human beings with the "you" we pronounce in addressing ourselves to him.

If it is true that because of the coming of Christ we can now address ourselves to God in a completely human way, we also know, however, that Jesus Christ is the only begotten Son of the Father, who in his greatness sustains our humanity. Therefore, when meditating it is important not to limit ourselves to searching for something that can be contemplated both within our hearts and outside of us. If we do this we shall end up submitting what we contemplate to the limitations of our viewpoint. On the contrary, we must allow God to have an absolutely free hand. He is the Altogether Different One, and we should let him be what he is, in total, confident silence. This silence, whether we call it emptiness or fullness, confidence or devotion, in the course of time, will transform our encounter with people and things. Thus, we will become capable of not forcing our ideas on others, and our life in common will become more human. "The more people become aware of themselves through silence, the more they find the way to arrive at the heart of their fellow human beings. A spouse, a co-worker, and a neighbor, become more understandable to us when we meditate about them," says Klemens Tilmann.

Inner silence, our ability to be silent, to listen, to pay attention, is not egotism or self-contemplation. The more we penetrate our own hearts, the more validly we shall find the way that leads to the hearts of our fellow human beings and to the mysterious depth of God. The often recalled inability of people of this modern age to believe comes from the fact that they lose the awareness of this depth. What value does it have for any Christian who wants to be transformed, to understand the truth theoretically but not be touched deep inside the heart? What strikes us about religious people is the fact that they have undergone a transformation in their hearts: they act inspired by an inner center that makes whatever they say believable.

Meditation as silence, as prayer before God, can reach such a depth that we become very solemn in our choice of words, even with the word "you." Alfons Rosenberg writes: "What is the exact meaning of being silent? Is it just being struck dumb, deliberately repressing one's words? . . . Does being silent mean renouncing the most human of all faculties, the word? Absolutely not. Authentic silence is not a denial or a loss or renunciation, since it opens the way to a world that is often at hand but mostly unknown, the way to the profound world of knowledge and love. By keeping silent we recover from destruction, we recall our energies back to their original sphere. By being silent, we ignite that inner recollection which—when it works—allows silence to develop. By being silent, we take the path that leads not only to other souls, but also to the depth of the world, and finally, to the depth of God."[3]

Therefore, we should not be afraid of abandoning ourselves to silence. Let us rejoice when, during the celebration of God's word and the Eucharist there are periods of silence between words. Our words must be real, they must rise from the depth and return once more to the depth. This is the liturgy, the celebration of God's mystery of salvation in our times. The same rules applied to the word hold true for singing. Singing can hardly be defined as prayer when it is only a way of hiding, of withdrawing from silence. Even the most exulting and most powerful song must spring from the silence of our heart.

It is not by thinking a lot but by loving a lot that we come close to God, says Teresa of Avila.[4] Teresa was not well-disposed towards those who were afraid and who suspected dangers everywhere, since we can, at any time, freely open ourselves to God in a silent, joyful wait. Both Teresa of Avila and John of the Cross teach that it is good to speak with God but that it is also good to stay in silence before him. In order to be close to those we love, it is not necessary to have their name constantly on our lips. It is possible for us to live with and in our fellow human beings and know them thoroughly without having to speak. In regard to this, Saint Paul uses a beautiful expression. He speaks of "God in whom we live and move and have our being" (Ac 17:28). Meditation grants us this silent intimacy, this silent union with God.

III. JESUS CHRIST: THE CENTER OF OUR MEDITATION

For us Christians, to meditate means to abandon ourselves to a love that is within ourselves and which also transcends us. This love has been revealed to us in Jesus Christ, in his relationship with God, whom he calls Father, and in his acting moved by the Spirit, which he promised shall be with us until the end of time. The relationship that Jesus had with those he encountered was determined by this love. Both for friends and enemies he represented a mystery they often did not understand. If the human closeness of Jesus had been enough to transmit the presence of God to his disciples, they would have not made this request: "Lord, teach us to pray" (Lk 11:1). Those who gathered around Jesus hoped to learn something about God from him, something about the meaning of life. They watched how he dedicated himself with infinite self-denial to the poor and the outcast, to the wise and the noble. They also saw him withdraw from the crowds in search of solitude to pray. They noticed that Jesus had a relationship with God that they lacked, but wished to have themselves. The disciples followed Jesus because they had a longing for truth. Yet, what a difficult task it was for Jesus to expand their hearts, moved by purely human feelings, to a love that does not seek its own interest but that reveals its power in the total renunciation of self.

Since the common life that the disciples led with Jesus was not enough to establish a living relationship with God, Jesus invited them to pray at all times and not to lose heart (cf. Lk 18:1). Jesus did not spare strengthening those who believed in him with the experience of his closeness to God. Let us consider the vision the disciples had on Mount Tabor (cf. Mk 9:2-10) and the breaking of the bread with the disciples at Emmaus (cf. Lk 24:13-15).

Tabor and Emmaus show us how God operates. On one hand, people suffer from disappointment, incomprehension and temptation to the point of extreme doubt; on the other hand, they experience this enormous closeness to God. The theological message of the Evangelists shows us the relationship there is between closeness and distance in the person of Jesus.

In meditation the person is interiorly touched by the reality of salvation; he or she is struck by a person; likewise, meditation is the means through which the mystery of Christ shines in every believer. The disciples who gathered around Jesus used to pray in the temple, sing hymns of praise, and meditate the texts of the scriptures. But their hearts longed for more. In Jesus of Nazareth, they perceived such strength, such silence and intensity of prayer, that they asked for his teaching. Jesus did not provide them a how-to manual for prayer. We only know a few passages that mention his dialogues with the Father.

Jesus meditated. He found rest in the secret of the Father. Creation itself, for him, was a sign of the Creator's goodness. The scriptures reveal his ability to meditate about nature, expressed also through his use of parables. Let us recall the parables of the sower, the shepherd, and the lilies of the fields, the grain of wheat that springs up, grows, and bears fruit. Let us also remember his references to the birds of the sky, the birds perched on the roofs, and to the hairs of our heads which are counted. In Jesus' contemplation, inner and outer realities were one and the same. What created unity was not the anonymous vibration of cosmic forces but the personal love of him who meditated, a love directed to every individual person, even to the smallest and most insignificant creature.

Following Jesus' example, the silence of meditation enables us to create space for a personal encounter. He who meditates, pauses, learns to wait, is tolerant, accepts all that exists, allows the others to talk through his silence, learns to listen and to pay attention. But meditation is not only the space in which love, the sensation of existing, the discovery of the "Other" becomes possible; meditation has already all that in itself. For those who believe, there is no separation between the hall and the inner court. God is close to those who are touched by Christ and persevere in being silent without thinking too much or resorting continuously to words, whether at work or at rest, in silence or speaking, in light or in darkness.

The Spanish mystic John of the Cross and the Oriental masters confirm this by explaining that there are two things that prevent people from seeing the truth: to think in a superficial way, and to lack inner vigilance. Christ assigned to us a hard itinerary.... He did not say: God will be closer to you whenever you feel happy, rather than when you are in darkness. Teresa of Avila and Thérèse of Lisieux knew how much our spiritual experience is subject to change, according to our different moods, since we are made of matter.

When a master in Oriental philosophies was asked in what way he had become famous and why so many people followed him, he answered: "During the first twenty years I remained completely unknown to the world. I exercised the *Zazen* and poverty; I had hardly enough food to eat; however, precisely thanks to the *Zen*, I was able to find a meaning to my life even in those circumstances."[1]

For the Christian, every practice of meditation is related to Christ. This relationship, whatever form of meditation it might take, cannot succeed without silence, without postponing temporarily one's own thoughts. When during meditation we allow the contemplated image to act silently over us, or when we listen attentively to the affirmations of the other, when we allow ourselves to be touched by the music or the words we have listened to, when we are rigidly seated—a position known not only in the East but also found in Christian monasticism—we must be interiorly silent. In fact, silence and stillness should always be correlated to affirmation, word, and form. Only when the form has in itself something of the creative silence from which it arises, does it guide us towards itself, towards the "Other," towards God.

PART TWO

DISCOVERING THE LIVES
OF RELIGIOUS PEOPLE

I. TERESA OF AVILA

1. HER PERSONALITY

Teresa of Avila is of interest to our contemporaries under many aspects. While she was an independent, gentle, and enterprising woman, filled with the strength of her faith, she was also human, merciful, and totally immersed in this world. She was endowed with great finesse and acute sensitivity to the problems of her days. Teresa educated herself continuously through her reading and talking to learned people. She used to question the superficial way of thinking of her generation, the enterprises of the Conquistadors, whose domains in the New World were often founded on blood and tears. Teresa did not leave the thinking to men, but she reflected together with them on their same level.

Teresa lived in a convent together with 150 sisters and had everything she could need — she led a comfortable and respectable life and maintained contacts with important people. However, she soon started to question the life that was led in the convent. She examined her life through the requests made by the gospel and the saints and discovered it did not conform to them. Her health was poor but her lively spirit dragged her weak body along with it. She got rid of some useless burdens which, as time went by, she had accumulated in the convent. To the astonishment of her sisters and superiors in the order, she founded a new convent, which was small and very poor. The bishop and some friends were the only ones to help her. A wise and pious Dominican barely managed to save Teresa's new foundation from the rage of the municipal council of the city of Avila. Weren't there already enough poor nuns in need of Spain's help in the sixteenth century? Was it really necessary for this Teresa de Ahumada to found, by her own will, an even poorer monastery? However, the reformation of the Carmelite order—which had remained unchanged until then—was only one aspect of Teresa's mission, the thrust of whose spiritual radiation went far beyond the monastic life.

Teresa's independence and inner vigilance shone forth in the way she dealt with matters related to her new foundation. She founded an order of strict cloister. In spite of her delicate health, she built her seventeen monasteries by travelling extensively along country roads in uncomfortable carts pulled by oxen. In those days, it was something exceptional for a woman to undertake such journeys. Teresa had to bear a lot of criticism and stand patiently many accusations. Sega, the papal nuncio, said about her: "Teresa is a restless little woman, she travels to and fro, and she is disobedient and stubborn. Under her religious appearance she brews false doctrines. In opposition to the precepts established by the Council of Trent and the order's superior, she has violated the cloister. She has taught as a professor of theology, even though Saint Paul says that women should not be allowed to teach."[1]

Teresa, however, was not intimidated. She interpreted Saint Paul with her own common sense. "Once," she writes, "while I was wondering whether those who were angry because of my founding journeys were right, and whether perhaps I should be occupied only with prayer, I heard these words being spoken to me: 'Do not worry in this life about having a more enjoyable life, but of fulfilling my will.' I have also thought about Saint Paul who speaks about the life of retirement that women should lead. This had been often told to me, even before I had read it and asked myself whether this was God's will. Then the Lord said to me: 'Tell them they should not base themselves on only one passage of the scriptures, but that they should also reflect on the others, if they do not wish to bind my hands.'"[2]

Teresa did not let her hands be bound. She found an ever growing number of friends, men and women, who after some initial distrust were conquered to the cause of God. With her gentleness, sharp intelligence, and humility, Teresa managed to disarm the Father provincial whom she had avoided during the foundation of her first convent, and who had summoned her to a court of the order.

Although it was not acknowledged at that time that women could give advice, Teresa believed that women could pass adequate judgments on different matters. Still, she suffered due to the lack of consideration that was given in their regard. The Inquisition had made great efforts in destroying all the awkward passages of her writings, but scholars were later able to reconstruct their meaning. In her book *The Way Of Perfection*, Teresa had written in this fashion: "God, you are not ungrateful, and I am certain that you listen to the prayer of us women. When you were here on earth, far from despising us you treated us with great kindness. You found that our love and faith were even greater than those you found in men.... Is it not enough, Lord, to be excluded from so many things in the world? There is nothing we can do for you in public, not even fling in its face its injustice.... Lord, you are a fair judge, not like the judges of this world who, as true sons of Adam and being men, are all suspect of every woman's virtue. Still, the day will come when they shall understand us all. I am not speaking for myself, since the world already knows my wretchedness, and I am glad it does. However, I think about our present times and I find it unfair that strong, serene, and confident hearts should be despised only because they belong to women."[3] In spite of the extreme conditioning factors from the outside, Teresa tried to find for herself and for her fellow human beings the answer they needed.

Where did Teresa find the strength to stand up for her autonomy and freedom? Where did she find the courage to tell the truth even under pressures and torments? Using today's language we could answer: from the fact that she meditated on a daily basis, from the fact that she immersed herself in the mystery of God. Teresa understood that a person is capable of giving oneself to another inasmuch as the person becomes one's true self. Teresa's whole life revolved around this "other" person she found in God. The process of becoming herself was no easy task for Teresa. We know that she had not been a religious person from birth. Although she belonged to a religiously oriented family, her joy of living and her pride could have led her along other ways. Before learning what prayer and personal dialogue with God meant, she reflected upon what she had seen and heard, trying to understand the meaning of such words as "eternity" and the "infinite." She had been told that God exists forever and that after dying, a person enters the eternity of God. This was her first experience of transcendence. The longing for this immensity fascinated her to such an extent that at the age of seven she secretly left home with one of her brothers in the hope to be killed by the Moors and reach that goal more speedily. But the earthly life too, attracted Teresa's flexible nature: she loved to flirt with her cousins, dress up, and use makeup. Evidently, Teresa wanted to have an impact upon people and be loved.

When Teresa first entered the convent she did not experience a lasting peace. She joined Carmel at the age of twenty-one, more as a result of her reflections than of her experience of God. She herself admits that what had driven her to take that step was the fear of hell rather than the love of God. This was certainly not the best motivation for entering the cloister. Teresa admits that even though in the order she was both loved and tried with many illnesses, which she patiently accepted, she tried to avoid God for almost twenty years. This may sound incredible, but it corresponds to her love of truth. Teresa perceived God's call but she was afraid, mortally afraid of abandoning herself to God in the way he expected of her. Before becoming capable, through her writings, of teaching others to pray, she had to experience herself what it meant to shun prayer and the preparation necessary for it. Like Saint Paul and

Saint Augustine, she experienced the inner conflict of her nature: she wanted what was good, but did what was evil.

For a long time Teresa found a hiding place in the official prayer of the Church, which consisted in reciting psalms in Latin and passages of the scriptures whose contents she did not understand. Moreover, she had to participate in numerous vocal prayers and attend countless liturgical functions. Like other Sisters, she had found a corner of her own to pray. Still, it wasn't Teresa's words that God wanted, but her heart; he wished to speak to her in the silence of meditation. Teresa called this conversation "inner prayer."

Inner prayer was for Teresa the experience we define today as "meditation." Teresa compared the process that takes place in outgrowing a state of superficial, learned prayer so as to become responsible individuals before God, to an interior agony. She encouraged those Christians who were going through this process to establish a personal relationship with God. The experience of God attained by Teresa of Avila, which made her an expert in prayer, did not consist so much in apparitions or extraordinary events, but rather in the experience of God's presence in the depth of the heart, a presence that can pervade one's entire being. She helps us realize that we become true persons only when we find God deep inside of ourselves.

While meditating one day on a painting of the scourging of Christ at the pillar, Teresa suddenly recognized her cowardice in not willing to face the divine adventure. After this experience, however, she lost her fear of being silent, of not using many words before God. Ever since then, she no longer felt abandoned to herself, to her doubts, and to her reflections. Instead, she turned her inner eyes to Christ, to

Jesus, the man. She did so not because of something she created in her imagination, but because she longed, in the dark, for the one who was close to her. Together with Saint Augustine she understood that God is closer to us than we are to ourselves. Urged by the Franciscan and Benedictine currents of spiritual thought, she introduced two hours of silent meditation into the daily schedule of her convents. For a nunnery, that was something unheard of. Teresa was judged as being presumptuous and was made to understand that women were not capable of engaging in such profound meditations. Fortunately, Teresa converted to her theses some theologians who took her side against the attacks made from within the order and from within the University of Salamanca. Several theologians admitted that Teresa had helped them to gain a new understanding of many theological problems.

With her teaching on prayer, Teresa of Avila released a dynamic force that strikes us deeply even today. Edith Stein, for example, was stimulated to conversion from reading her works. However, a person cannot reach one's innermost depth without a personal effort. To meditate we must fulfill an exercise which, through continuous repetition, recalls our attention to the voice of consciousness, to the answer that comes from deep inside, and to listening to the word of God. In order to proclaim one's faith, it is not enough to simply listen to the word of God. Our listening has to become action. The action, in turn, creates a space for silence, which renders possible our attention and love towards our neighbor.

Only a truly accomplished person knows how to use silence, to establish the right time to its exercise in discovering one's own identity and who God and neighbor are. Teresa was deeply interested in the matter of our self-fulfillment, which enables us to authentically bear witness to God. She dedicated her life to this cause, taking upon herself, besides the foundation of the convents, the toil of her literary work.

Teresa's humanity developed through her sensitivity to God and through her awareness of the needs of others. A niece says of her: "My aunt was filled with such life and spontaneity that people could not believe how saintly she was."[4] Jerome Gracian, the first provincial of the Teresian foundations, writes: "Her gentle, cordial, and pleasant manner attracted everyone who knew her and had any dealings with her, and everyone loved her. She detested the severe and surly manner of some saints, who thus made both themselves and perfection unappealing."[5] Teresa lived the natural sanctity of the gospel. In imitating Jesus she tried to behave affectionately and simply with people of every condition and personality.

Teresa not only prayed often and at length but was also a lovable business-woman, always ahead of everybody in dealings related to lands, buildings, and properties. One day, on a visit to a friend who belonged to the nobility of Madrid, some courtesans who were curious to see the Mother foundress, gathered at the hostess' house. When Teresa entered the room, those who were present heard nothing but her joyful exclamation: "My God, how beautiful the streets in Madrid are!"[6] The Franciscan nuns, whom Teresa visited immediately after, were fascinated by her humanity and later reported: "Praise God who allows us to see a saint whom we can all imitate. She talks, sleeps, and eats like anyone else and is neither too solemn nor too sweet."[7]

Those who would like to know about Teresa of Avila's fascinating spontaneity should read her letters. Along with her profound spiritual exhortations, there are passages seasoned with exquisite spirit, which reveal an ability to understand and love other people. "I believe I shall be less disturbed here. I am in a hermitage from where I can see the river even from my bed. It is a view that gives me great joy. Today I am feeling better than usual."[8] "I have always been very imperfect. I believe that I am now even more entitled to look after myself because I feel old and exhausted. You would be amazed if you saw me. That day I was having pangs of hunger, so the walnuts arrived at the right time. I still have some you have sent me here. They are very good. Eat, then, the rest of them out of love for me."[9] "I attribute great value to the virtues, but not to rigor. This can be seen in all our houses. Maybe it is because I am still not ready to do penance."[10] "Our Mother prioress will tell you how happy I am for the state [of matrimony] that God has given you for your happiness. May you live in that state at his service, because there are saints among those who are married as in every state of life. You too can become one of them, if you do not fail through your own fault."[11]

In Teresa's life and work we see that a person becomes a personality inasmuch as he or she enters into contact with the visible and invisible truth of the surrounding world. A typical characteristic of Teresa's was that once she had established a personal relationship with God, she did not repress but accepted reality with all its implications, examining and guiding the reactions of her heart and thoughts. Like any human being, she also had her weaknesses, which she did not try to conceal but openly acknowledged. One of these behavioral weaknesses consisted in a certain existential fear which was particularly related to the role of women in those days. More than once, Teresa corrected through her deeds recurrent affirmations such as: "We are poor, weak women, who can do no good."

2. THE SPIRITUAL EXPERIENCE

I. Teresa of Avila and John of the Cross

Sometimes we hear that Teresian christological mysticism is beyond criticism, whereas in John of the Cross it has been noted that there lies a tendency to withdraw from any use of images in meditation, or at least to attribute less importance to them. This is where the comparison with Eastern meditation enters in, and it should be critically valued. It is true that Teresa of Avila, in spite of her friendship with John of the Cross, criticized his introduction of radical "Carthusian spirituality" into the Carmelite order. However, in spite of all the differences that existed in the personalities and education of both mystics, their affirmations agree on the essential points.

For a deeper assessment of their teachings, perhaps we can resort to the studied concepts that deal with active and passive outlooks of theology. In agreement with Dionysius the Areopagite, in her book *Ways To the Knowledge Of God*, Edith Stein asserts that the way to approach God is different for each individual, but on the peak of the knowledge of God every path converges in divine darkness, in which for the human spirit there is no longer message or distinction.[1] Naturally, this should not be interpreted in Dionysius as syncretism—as if the religion to which we belong is indifferent—but rather as method.

Otger Steggink OCD, is certainly right to assert in *Experience And Realism In Teresa of Avila And John of the Cross* that as an answer to the rationalistic exercise of science and the dulled preaching of the faith at that time, Teresa emphasized the need of the religious experience, thus converting many, even theologians, to a life of meditation and interior prayer. On the other hand, not only the poems of Saint John of the Cross but also his prose, though less expressive, are sustained by a profound spiritual experience that reveals the harmony between thought and experience in his life.

The mysticism of John of the Cross is determined by the same Orthodox Christology of Teresa of Avila, but there are many aspects dealt with by Teresa, such as meditating on a painting, for which John does not waste a single word. Although, like Teresa, he did meditate on images, whenever the meditation became more profound he abandoned his reflections in order to spend time with God, keeping himself empty and deprived of images. This tendency can also be seen in Teresa, but in a way more befitting to her own nature. Since her education had not been directed towards reasoning, what prevailed in her was a thinking process based on images, a process she uses to explain her spiritual way. She compares the innermost part of the person to a unique painting of many colors: a magnificent castle with innumerable rooms.

For both mystics, this is ultimately the deepest level of the soul, the center of the human person's depth in Jesus Christ. Both maintain that only those who reach their own depth through prayer are capable of reaching fulfillment in faith and in turn can enrich others through their own experience.

Teresa of Avila writes in *The Interior Castle*: "Let us consider that this castle has, as I said, many dwelling places: some up above, others down below, others to the sides; and in the center and middle is the main dwelling place where the very secret exchanges between God and the soul take place. It's necessary that you keep this comparison in mind."[2] Teresa highlights the symbolism of her image. Immediately after, she compares the entire castle to an Oriental pearl, a transparent crystal in whose center God dwells as a sun that radiates everything.[3] John of the Cross also uses the image of the sun.[4]

The actions of every man and woman who has been created for such glory are useless if their deeds "do not proceed from that principle, which is God."[5] For Teresa of Avila the small efforts made by us Christians in our good words or prayers are not enough; as John of the Cross, she demands much more: total commitment, at least as a goal that we must have constantly before our eyes. The first cause, the depth, the innermost part of the soul, are the terms she uses when she exhorts us to reflect upon our life and our relationship with God.

While John of the Cross speaks about being deprived and empty, Teresa of Avila speaks of love for the cross; while he speaks of consolation and peace, she describes how God expands our human heart and makes it rejoice. Both agree on the fact that our relationship with God, whose presence we become aware of through meditation, can only be conceived in utmost stillness, that is, in profound silence.

II. Water as a symbol of contemplation

During the twenty years of painful struggle it took to find God in meditation, Teresa attempted to find an image which would indicate the different accesses to God, the first cause. Because she had a special predilection for water, and since hydraulic energy was exploited at her time, she used two comparisons which she found before her eyes. In her autobiography she describes four different methods that can be used to water a garden. First, by drawing the water from a well, which takes great effort. Second, by furnishing the wells with wheel and drawing devices; thus, a greater amount of water can be drawn with less effort compared to the previous system. The third method is to convey water from a stream or river to the garden by means of channels. Compared to the other watering methods the latter makes things enormously easier for the gardener. The fourth and last method, which is particularly important for Teresa, is to water the garden by means of a plentiful rainfall. In this case a person's work and the mechanical means are no longer necessary. God himself takes care of everything.[6]

In her writings about her experiences with God, Teresa tries to outline this gift that comes from above. All the aids Teresa devised for herself such as life within the order and the daily schedule, have one aim: to make one sensitive to the silent, gentle, pacifying, and blessed encounter with God.

Teresa tries to fix this experience in our minds by means of a second image: "Let's consider, for a better understanding, that we see two founts with two water troughs.... These two troughs are filled with water in different ways; with one the water comes from far away through many aqueducts and the use of much ingenuity; with the other the source of the water is right there, and the trough fills without any noise. If the spring is abundant, as is this one we are speaking about, the water overflows once the trough is filled, forming a large stream. There is no need of any skill, nor does the building of aqueducts have to continue.... The water coming from the aqueducts is comparable, in my opinion, to the consolations I mentioned that are drawn from meditation. For we obtain them through thoughts, assisting ourselves, using creations to help our meditation, and tiring the intellect. Since, in the end, the consolation comes through our own efforts, noise is made when there has to be some replenishing of the benefits the consolation causes in the soul, as has been said."[7]

Therefore, Teresa of Avila is also familiar with the principles of a passive approach in theology. As John of the Cross says, by tiring ourselves out with our reflections and the analyses of things, we shall not be able to attain the inner joy that springs from our closeness to God. During our meditation, our thoughts must keep silence. In comparison to John of the Cross, Teresa of Avila expresses herself in a way that is more elegant, richer in images, but also less systematic. Her method must be deduced from the flow of thoughts. Teresa attributes great importance to the second basin. She continues: "With this other fount, the water comes from its own source which is God. And since His Majesty desires to do so—when He is pleased to grant some supernatural favor—He produces this delight with the greatest peace and quiet and sweetness in the very interior part of ourselves. I don't know from where or how, nor is that happiness and delight experienced, as are earthly consolations, in the heart. I mean there is no similarity at the beginning, for afterward the delight fills everything; this water overflows through all the dwelling places and faculties until reaching the body. That is why I said that it begins in God and ends in ourselves. For, certainly, as anyone who may have experienced it will see, the whole exterior man enjoys this spiritual delight and sweetness."[8]

In this passage Teresa presents a synthesis of her mystical message, which agrees not only with the experience and needs of Saint John of the Cross but also with our own contemporary meditative process that invites people to deep interior silence, to being with oneself and with God. God, the prime mover, is the water spring in the analogy of the fountains. It is typical of the spring to deliver its water "without the noise" of artificial mechanisms; metaphorically meaning: without the noise of our thoughts. The spring supplies its water "immediately"—this is another of

Teresa's favorite words. A person's longing is quenched only when one can grasp at once the object of one's longing, not through the use of numerous figurative meditations that can only cause disturbance.

The water of divine manifestation always flows full of "sweetness," in "tranquillity," "from the depth of the soul," towards heaven. It is not easy to imagine water flowing upwards. Still, water is only an image for Teresa. Also Jesus uses this image: "Let him drink who believes in me.... From within him rivers of living water shall flow" (Jn 7:38). Teresa was particularly familiar with this passage from the scriptures. Significantly, she adds: "without knowing where or how [this happens]." Even those laws and limitations that obstruct our human horizons crumble. Precisely because they come from the innermost region of the soul, beatitude and joy in our perception of transcendence are different from the transient joys we experience in observing other creatures. This interior joy pervades "a person as a whole" without excluding any part of one's existence.

Therefore, contemplation is not—considered dualistically—a pure spiritual experience that neglects our body; on the contrary, the latter participates in the experience without disturbing our spirit. The person in his or her entirety is wrapped and pervaded by an infinite meekness and gentleness in the encounter. John of the Cross attempts to describe this in the following terms: "O You, then, delicate touch, the Word, the Son of God, through the delicacy of your Divine being, You subtly penetrate the substance of my soul.... O, then, very delicate, exceedingly delicate, touch of the Word, so much the more delicate for me insofar as, after overthrowing the mountains and smashing the rocks to pieces on Mount Horeb... You gave the prophet the sweetest and strongest experience of Yourself in the gentle breeze! (3 K 19:11-12)."[9]

III. The dimension of depth

Teresa corrects herself often since, after all, there is no image that can adequately describe these processes. "I was now thinking while writing this," she explains, "that the verse mentioned above *Dilatasti cor meum*, says the heart was expanded. I don't think the experience is something, as I say, that rises from the heart, but from another part still more interior, as from something deep. I think this must be the center of the soul.... For certainly I see secrets within ourselves that have often caused me to marvel."[10]

From her words we understand that the point is not, as it often happens today, to have the heart and the center of our body compete as the place where meditation happens. For example, it is said that in the "lower region of the primitive origin," there lies, in fact, the body's center of gravity, but not the center of the spirit.[11]

Teresa of Avila and John of the Cross see this inner center in a depth whose intimacy and profoundness cannot be sufficiently grasped. This innermost region experienced in meditation, is not opposed to the sphere of our heart. Teresa of Avila's experience can be compared to several medieval or older paintings of Christ. The artists were directly aware of this relationship. In Christ, who often appears seated in an almond-shaped halo, artists used to highlight the center of his body, not the area of his heart. Under the richness of the folds his body resembles a wheel. The same phenomenon can be observed in the representations of Mary.

Compared to John of the Cross, as it has been said, Teresa of Avila usually expresses herself more indirectly, thus her language has a more personal quality to it, even if John of the Cross thinks in a similarly personal way. Teresa, for example, does not say, "abandon yourselves," "stay calm," "silent," but: "Every way in which the Lord helps the soul here, and all He teaches it, takes place with such quiet and so noiselessly that, seemingly to me, the work resembles the building of Solomon's temple where no sound was heard. So in this temple of God, in this His dwelling place, He alone and the soul rejoice together in the deepest silence. There is no reason for the intellect to stir or seek anything, for the Lord who created it wishes to give it repose here and that through a small crevice it might observe what is taking place. At times this sight is lost and the other faculties do not allow the intellect to look, but this happens for only a very short time. In my opinion, the faculties are not lost here; they do not work, but remain as though in amazement. I am amazed as well to see that when the soul arrives here all raptures are taken away."[12]

Above all, Teresa of Avila describes meditation as a gift, a correspondence that takes place in silence. What she experiences happens "in silence," in "great peace," and so on. To learn the method, we have to be willing to be alone or to look for solitude. However, equally important for her is our engaging in spiritual conversation with friends, in which our experiences are exchanged, and she submits this to the criteria of the scriptures and theological knowledge. As John of the Cross emphasizes, in the dimension of depth thoughts and reflections are disturbing. The intellect may develop its activity at any other time, but not during meditation.

Peace, being with oneself and with God, is not an end in itself whose purpose is to embellish the souls of those who distance themselves from less fortunate people. Teresa of Avila thinks in a realistic way; she wants to fulfill Christ's life in its totality, not only partially. She writes to her Sisters: "I repeat, it is necessary that your foundation consist of more than prayer and contemplation. If you do not strive for the virtues and practice them, you will always be dwarfs.... I hold that love, where present, cannot possibly be content with remaining always the same."[13] For Teresa, to possess the virtues means to develop our spiritual forces, to be active, to serve our neighbor, both inside and outside the cloister.

In accordance with John of the Cross, Teresa of Avila affirms that the more a person arrives at the depth of one's soul and the sooner he or she abandons the external images—even the best image of the soul and of God is neither the soul nor God—the more seldom shall one experience extraordinary phenomena through changes in the state of consciousness or the action of grace. Teresa of Avila and John of the Cross underline that visions, interior locutions, and emerging images do not belong to the most intimate experiences. The person who prays should not attribute great value to them and should let them pass by. Since, because of the Inquisition, Teresa did not have access to certain literature and formation material and suffered partly due to the inadequacy of some spiritual counselors, she was grateful for the times she found support in the image of the risen Christ in her heart.

IV. Identity

Teresa of Avila and John of the Cross describe the graces of our becoming aware of God's presence in the depth of our soul in connection with the experience of our indestructible identity. Peace and interior joy are the assets of those who meditate, which enable them to cope with their everyday problems. The cross does not fail those who pray, Teresa says, "it doesn't disquiet or make them lose peace. For the storms, like a wave, pass quickly. And the fair weather returns, because the presence of the Lord they experience makes them soon forget everything."[14]

"Courage" and "determination" are two of the favorite words used by Teresa of Avila. The spirit of the Conquistadors—to whom her own brothers belonged—was likewise alive in her, but on another level. Teresa also reached out to many people whose religiosity had stiffened into a routine Christianity. It sounds like a war-cry when she writes: "This is the reason of prayer . . . : the birth always of good works, good works."[15]

For Teresa of Avila, the fruits that spring from true meditation and contemplation consist in imitating the Crucified in order to become "servants of God," in committing one's life and offering oneself for the salvation of one's fellow human beings. "You must not think, Sisters, that the effects I mentioned are always present in these souls.... For sometimes our Lord leaves these individuals in their natural state.... True, this natural state lasts only a short while, a day at most or a little more. And in this great disturbance, usually occasioned by some event, the soul's gain through the good company it is in becomes manifest. For the Lord gives the soul great stability and good resolutions not to deviate from His service in anything... our Lord does not want the soul to forget its being, so that... it might always be humble."[16]

For Teresa of Avila, true peace and tranquility are Christ, the Lord himself. The individual that believes and rests in contemplation knows to be close to Jesus, whose friendship sustains and strengthens him or her. Teresa uses again the image of the castle with many rooms to illustrate the relationship between the depth of a person's soul and one's other faculties: "What, do you think, is the reason for those inspirations... I mentioned, and those messages the soul sends from the interior center to the people at the top of the castle and to the dwelling places outside the center where it is? Is it so that those outside might fall asleep? No, absolutely not! That the faculties, senses, and all the corporeal will not be idle, the soul wages more war from the center than it did when it was outside suffering with them, for then it didn't understand the tremendous gain trials bring. Perhaps they were the means by which God brought it to the center, and the company it has gives it much greater strength than ever."[17]

Those who live on the strength of prayer defeat suffering.

Their life is supported by the strength of God. "For if here below, as David says, in the company of the saints we will become saints, there is no reason to doubt that, being united with the Strong One through so sovereign a union of spirit with spirit, fortitude will cling to such a soul; and so we shall understand what fortitude the saints had for suffering and dying.... This is what I want us to strive for, my Sisters; and let us desire and be occupied in prayer not for the sake of our enjoyment but so as to have this strength to serve."[18]

The ultimate goal is not our works, but our pursuit of love, our inner disposition. People are often denied outstanding ventures; in fact, their daily life is rather modest. Still, everything that is included in contemplation can hold true for them. "We shouldn't build castles in the air. The Lord doesn't look so much at the greatness of our works as at the love with which they are done. And if we do what we can, His Majesty will enable us each day to do more and more, provided that we do not quickly tire. But during the little while this life lasts—and perhaps it will last a shorter time than each one thinks—let us offer the Lord interiorly and exteriorly the sacrifice we can. His Majesty will join it with that which He offered on the cross to the Father for us. Thus even though our works are small they will have the value our love for Him would have merited had they been great."[19]

As a firm teacher in spirituality, Teresa of Avila does not hesitate to admonish those who pray but never use violence in their innermost self, even when they come across obstacles. People do not really have control over themselves. They must always resort to the help of others, especially God's. Teresa called this knowledge of one's own condition humility. The great joy that stems from the experience of inner certainty described by Paul when he says: "Who will separate us from the love of Christ?" (Rom 8:35), cannot go unheard; Teresa of Avila adds: "Once you get used to enjoying this castle, you will find rest in all things, even those involving much labor, for you will have the hope of returning to the castle which no one can take away from you."[20]

II. JOHN OF THE CROSS

1. SPIRITUAL DIRECTION

Unlike our present times, the practice of the religious profession in the sixteenth century carried a tone of social instability. The priesthood was held in great esteem though at the same time marred due to its association with the structures of power. Even those belonging to religious orders were not fully guaranteed the necessary conditions to lead a meaningful religious life.

John of the Cross, a contemporary of Teresa of Avila, met the order's foundress in 1567 and informed her about his idea of becoming a Carthusian monk. As it had happened to Teresa, John of the Cross was disturbed by some habits that had developed in religious orders at that time. While John, according to his inclination, sought among the Carthusians a true monastic life, Teresa's aim was to create a new way in which, to her judgment, silence, spirit of prayer, and true fraternal love could be found, the same things John hoped to find by changing order. John was greatly impressed by Teresa, who convinced him that it was his task to initiate the reform of the men's Carmelite order, while she would found the women's reformed houses. Both stressed a revival of discipleship of Christ, an internalizing of spiritual life, an escaping from a more or less superficial ecclesiastical activity.

John of the Cross made up for his general lack of spiritual orientation by studying the holy scriptures and concerning himself with the tradition of the Church and the social needs of his time. Teresa of Avila had shown him that an intense life with Christ in prayer and silence cannot be separated from contact with our fellow human beings, who at all times long for true spiritual guidance. In 1568, at the age of twenty six, with the assistance of a Brother who shared his beliefs, John of the Cross founded, in extreme poverty, a reformed monastery in Durvelo, northern Spain. At that time one of his first initiatives was to announce the word of God in the neighboring villages.

John of the Cross became the co-founder of the Teresian reform, which gave an answer particularly to the evangelical command of poverty and to the love of both God and neighbor. Still, John of the Cross did not abandon the monastery. On the contrary, he attempted to fill the traditional forms of monastic life in the Carmel with new Christian values. Critical periods such as the sixteenth and twentieth centuries do not only bring about decadence, but also a new beginning, the onset of life-filled tendencies that give rise to long-expected reforms in the practices of the Church conditioned by the period. Due to their active intervention in matters that troubled their times, John of the Cross and Teresa of Avila unintentionally became the main representatives of Spanish mysticism.

In order to renew the Christian life and give new

meaning to priestly service, John of the Cross withdrew from a life directed to consumerism to take in earnest the words of Jesus: "It is easier for a camel to pass through a needle's eye than for a rich man to enter the kingdom of God" (Mt 19:24). Thus, he led a life of poverty, without seeking benefits, honors, or dignities. Throughout his life as a monk he was entrusted with different offices, both in individual monasteries and in presiding over the order. Still, he did not use this to increase his prestige, but as a challenge to be more seriously committed to carry the cross of Christ. How scarcely the reformed Carmelite branch took to this spirit of Christ can be seen by the fate suffered by John of the Cross before his death. He was not only imprisoned in Toledo due to the antagonism of some of his former Brothers, but also suffered the hostility of his own order. At the age of forty nine, after having been dismissed as superior, some wanted him expelled from the order for his opposition to the lust for power of his superiors. Between bodily and spiritual threats, John writes: "Where there is no love, put love and you will draw out love."[1]

Are we not scandalized today by the self-denial and austerity of John of the Cross? Wouldn't we rather talk about maturity and humanism than about carrying the cross? This may be understandable since self-discipline and the cross are concepts that have been long overstressed in our educational system, without considering the fact that only mature people are capable of suffering and carrying a burden. We cannot expect the same things from everybody alike: John of the Cross based his work on spiritual guidance, according to the inclination of each individual; he was meek and full of understanding in his judgments. For

John of the Cross, mystical ascent or self-discipline did not mean fundamentally the mortification of the flesh or blind obedience, but rather continuous prayer and assistance offered to our neighbor. He dedicated endless hours to those who sought counsel, for which several Brothers of less wisdom accused him of not observing the daily schedule a superior was supposed to follow, and of not living up to his vow of obedience. John made religion attractive and his behavior was neither rude nor tiresome but filled with concern for his neighbors. Since before entering the order he had worked as a nurse in a hospital, as priest and superior he willingly looked after the sick. During the construction of the monasteries he helped as a bricklayer and designed the aqueducts. He remained united through love to his family, which lived in great poverty, and helped them whenever he could. John of the Cross, whose outward appearance was that of a small and modest man, and who went unnoticed most of the time, left an indelible impression on others for his humanity and fraternal love, and for his intense life of prayer; many were those whom he showed the way leading to God.

John of the Cross used to become severe and inflexible when it came to the method to be used in prayer. He was outraged by the false guidance given by some spiritual directors which he believed did not satisfy the human thirst for God. Their methods of spiritual counseling were directed to prevail over the faithful in order to force them to accept their own viewpoints, rather than paying attention to the way in which the spirit of God wished to act in each individual. John of the Cross did not want to cram people's minds with many pious thoughts, and gave greater value to helping people achieve inner peace. It was more important that they learn how to *listen* to God rather than to *tell* him something. His sensitivity gave him the ability to understand the reawakening of people's personal needs.

Influenced by German mysticism, Greek traditional thinking about the couple archetype relationship gave way to the image of a relationship of friendship between God and the soul.

Teresa of Avila, Ignatius of Loyola and John of the Cross were imbued with that relationship. Our relationship with God is now basically structured on our being face to face with him, no longer on our ascent of the steps of being.[2] John of the Cross was opposed to the imposition of traditional schemes upon those who sought for help. Like the German mystics he too was convinced that God dwelled deep inside the human person; thus, it is necessary to keep silence, in order to acquire the awareness of his presence.

People are driven to do things, to act, to produce. According to John of the Cross, meditation — which he identified as contemplation — consists in receiving, in listening. God and the person meet like lovers who can be close to each other more by keeping silence than by speaking. Therefore, it is understandable why the saint was indignant whenever he came across people who were led in the opposite direction by false teachings: "A spiritual director will happen along who, like a blacksmith, knows no more than how to hammer and pound with the faculties. Since hammering with the faculties is this director's only teaching, and he knows no more than how to meditate, he will say: 'Come, now, lay aside these rest periods, which amount to idleness and a waste of time; take and meditate and make interior acts, for it is necessary that you do your part; this other method is the way of illusions and typical of fools.' "[3]

John of the Cross kept far from denying the soul's ability to think, act, and meditate on the word of God. In almost every page of his works we come across the words of the scripture. Thérèse of Lisieux learned from him to take the Bible in earnest. For John of the Cross, our current understanding of silent meditation is included in the notion of contemplation, which does not mean inactivity but "communication, that is, the means to attain Salvation and Redemption."[4] "These directors should reflect that they themselves are not the chief agent, guide, and mover of souls in this matter, but that the principal guide is the Holy Spirit, Who is never neglectful of souls, and that they are instruments for directing them to perfection through faith.... Thus the director's whole concern should not be to accommodate souls to his own method and condition, but he should observe the road along which God is leading them, and if he does not recognize it, he should leave them alone and not bother them."[5]

John of the Cross had a profound respect for the human person. His favorite words were "silence" and "freedom of spirit." "Directors should strive to disencumber the soul and bring it into solitude and idleness so that it may not be tied to any particular knowledge, earthly or heavenly, or to any covetousness for some satisfaction or pleasure, or to any other apprehension, in such a way that it may be empty through the pure negation of every creature, and placed in spiritual poverty. This is what the soul must do...."[6] This lack of action is not quietism but something that stems from an extremely active source, from the use of the entire will. People are capable of retreating deep inside themselves in silence; they can become detached and empty of all impressions in order to approach that mystery experienced by John of the Cross that reaches beyond the comprehensible and explicable. "Negation of every creature" does not mean to draw far from creation to meet the Creator but to listen attentively to him in the peace of our hearts. "God, like the sun, stands above souls ready to communicate Himself."[7] People who are imprisoned by things, in the noise of their own knowledge, are blind to the shining sun that keeps every creature alive.

Today more than ever, in this world dominated by technology, people crave for a deeper dimension of life that appears concealed to them. They search for teachers but cannot find them. Only few have the courage to be silent and free themselves from superficial things. Only few, like John of the Cross, encourage and take the hand of those who search for God: "Let yourself go, silence your thoughts, be calm and quiet. Don't be afraid, I am coming along with you."

John of the Cross walked with his fellow human beings along their paths. What is guidance if not the possibility of being together, which consists not only in teaching, but first of all in acting with others, in communicating life.

2. PERSONAL MEDITATION

I. Allowing ourselves to be transported

In his book *Ascent to Mount Carmel*, John of the Cross says: "Some souls, instead of abandoning themselves to God and cooperating with Him, hamper Him by their indiscreet activity or resistance. They resemble children who kick and cry, and struggle to walk by themselves when their mothers want to carry them; in walking by themselves they make no headway, or if they do, it is at a child's pace."[1]

The master of silence, who teaches us how to search deep inside our heart, uses this concrete image to tell us what is often lacking in us and which are our mistakes when we immerse ourselves in prayer. Perhaps we are familiar with the words of the holy Curate of Ars, who tells us about what an old village farmer answered when he was asked why he spent so many hours in church: "I watch God and God watches me." Undoubtedly, the prayer of this simple man was the type of prayer John of the Cross had in mind in guiding others to attain faith in God and a confident devotion towards him. But how can we find today such a way to master serenity and confidence in prayer?

The tragic side of those Christians who often take so much trouble to do things is that in their personal relationship with God they behave like children, whereas in other aspects of life they undergo a normal process of maturation. This childish behavior has nothing to do with what

the Evangelists or Saint Paul call the purpose of one's relationship with God; that is, to be and behave like God's
children.

We cannot merely place our religious activity alongside
the rest of our activities. To pray does not mean to switch
from one activity to another. In becoming aware of God's
closeness, in meditating, in establishing an internal dialogue
with him, we enter a dimension that is deeper than that in
which we usually find ourselves. We must switch from the
field of doing to that of allowing, of letting ourselves go,
of staying quiet, which does not mean being idle.

Let us return to the comparison used by John of the
Cross: a child in its mother's arms can do many things. He
or she can be interiorly alert, can watch, feel, and
experience closeness. The child does not have to determine
what direction to follow, but be confident that the goal will
be reached by letting oneself be carried. Every person
should understand that in this world one cannot reach the
ultimate goal alone, but only with the assistance of a deeper
relationship with one's Creator. Experience is a necessary
contribution to every Christian's maturity: God is neither a
scarecrow nor a landlord that demands payment of our
debts. He is a mystery into which we must enter
confidently. All words that are spoken within God's silence,
enter through this very silence into a deeper dimension.
According to John of the Cross, people must not create a
God for themselves by reflecting or meditating but enter
that mystery in which God reveals and gives himself as he
is.

There is no calculation, no knowing beforehand in our
abandoning ourselves to God. A person who meditates,

often sees nothing, feels nothing, knows nothing, and still notices that in this obscure confidence one is closer to God than when guided by the small light of personal knowledge. "A person should take note that even though he does not seem to be making any progress in this quietude or doing nothing, he is advancing much faster than if he were treading along on foot, for God is carrying him. Although he is walking at God's pace, he does not feel this pace.... It is no wonder if he does not advert to this, for the senses do not attain to what God effects in the soul at this time. As the Wise Man says: *The words of wisdom are heard in silence.* [Ec 9:17] A soul, then, should abandon itself into God's hands and not its own."[2]

The same things are upheld by a Japanese Christian, a follower of John of the Cross: "Saint John Damascene refers to this attitude of the soul when he says that to pray is to offer our heart to God. On the other hand, other definitions of prayer such as 'Dialogue with God' (Saint Augustine), 'Elevation of the soul to God' (Saint Gregory Nicene), 'Speaking to God as to an intimate friend' (Saint Teresa of Avila), would seem to refer rather to the external aspects of prayer. In fact, in trying to reach an internal definition we understand that to pray means 'to remain silent before God' rather than 'to talk to God.' And rather than 'to raise both our minds and hearts to God,' to pray means to plunge ourselves and immerse ourselves in God, both in soul and in body; that is, our whole being."[3]

II. Being silent

John of the Cross acknowledged the value of interior silence. In order to define silence he uses terms such as: letting ourselves be transported, emptying ourselves, not seeing, believing. In the language used by Teresa of Avila this means: "God wants our heart to be empty, pure and longing for his consolation."⁴ There are other concepts in both saints that are similar to these, like having peace, not doing, going into depth. These attitudes constitute the active contribution provided by those who pray. The more we move away from the activity of the senses directed towards the outside, the more responsive we become to the action of the Holy Spirit deep inside our heart. The senses are the shell that those who pray must break in order to reach complete maturity in Christ. "Should a person always have attachment to them and never become detached, he would never stop being a little child, or speaking of God as a child, or knowing and thinking of God as a child. In his attachment to the rind of sense (the child), he will never reach the substance of spirit (the perfect man)... a child must be weaned in order to accustom its palate to a hardier and more substantial diet."⁵

This nutritious food consists in attaining inner silence, in allowing ourselves to be guided by God's spirit. John of the Cross ironically remarks: "I greatly fear what is happening in these times of ours: If any soul whatever after a bit of meditation has in its recollection one of these locutions, it will immediately baptize all as coming from God and with such a supposition say, 'God told me,' 'God answered me.' Yet this is not so, but, as we pointed out, these persons themselves are more often the origin of their locution."[6]

Religious naiveté is something found not only in the sixteenth century but even today. The imitation of Christ, self-denial, being available to our neighbor, can be easily transformed into emotional euphoria, in which the person who prays speaks with God as if the latter were a common man whose shoulders could be patted on. The profusion of words and the experience of certain sensations do not necessarily imply the existence of a genuine relationship with God. Despite our closeness to the Father, which Christ has taught us, we cannot forget that there is a reverential distance between ourselves and God. We cannot cancel the fact that the divine Person is a being totally different from us. We can become aware of this distance by keeping silent, by experiencing the difference between God and ourselves and by regularly training ourselves in this attitude. Our spontaneous conversation with God should be sustained by our disposition to grow in our awareness of his closeness to us, in understanding who God is and who we are.

Like many teachers of spiritual life such as Dionigi, Eckhart, Tauler and Teresa of Avila, John of the Cross underlines the importance of practicing inner silence. This silence is connected with the words of Christ, urging us not to use too many words in prayer (cf. Mt 6:7). "When His disciples asked Him to teach them to pray, Christ obviously, as one Who knew so well his Father's will, would have told them all that was necessary in order to obtain an answer from the Eternal Father; and, in fact, He only told them those seven petitions of the *Pater Noster*, which include all our spiritual and temporal necessities.... He told them that in praying they should not desire much speaking."[7]

III. Becoming quiet

It is often said that the Christian should not seek consolations or sweetness in prayer. Christ fulfilled the Redemption on the cross; therefore, the mark of a true Christian is the capacity to endure suffering. The truth contained in this statement is illustrated in the words of the saints. This is already true in the natural order of love: the person who in one's partner or friend seeks only comfort is a selfish person, trying to please oneself rather than the other person. Despite this, the following must be said: "Whatever is decisive needs neither to be done nor endured... since what has already happened on the part of God is more important than what may or not happen through us."[8] References about the search for comfort and joy in God also prevail in the teachings of the spiritual leaders. Since God is light, joy, and peace, we can experience him also in this manner. The fact that God is also experienced as darkness, absence, and aridity does not stem from him but from human nature, which is weak and poorly receptive. In order to change this pattern, an adequate introduction to prayer and an exercise proper to each situation is necessary.

John of the Cross walks hand in hand with those who search, starting from the basics, from his understanding of the human person. "God," he says, "to achieve His work gently and to lift the soul to supreme knowledge, must begin by touching the low state and extreme of the senses. And from there He must gradually bring the soul after its own manner to the other end, spiritual wisdom, which is incomprehensible to the senses. Thus, naturally or supernaturally, He brings a person to the supreme spirit of God by first instructing him through discursive meditation and through forms, images, and sensible means, according to the individual's own manner of acquiring knowledge."[9]

When it comes to our spiritual life, John, just like Teresa, is a supporter of repetition and exercise. Both underline the fact that in every individual, the disposition towards God and God's action are two different things. Therefore, no rigid rule can be established. For John it is decisive to quiet our hearts and educate them to tranquility: "Our nature is so unstable and fragile that even when well disciplined it will hardly fail to stumble upon thoughts with the memory; and these thoughts become a disturbance to a soul that was residing in peace and tranquility through the forgetfulness of all."[10]

We cannot expect to draw any illumination or transformation from prayer unless God himself supplies it. It is already no small thing for the learner to gather the courage to find outer and inner peace through prayer and to be ready to welcome God's action. "It would be to your advantage to remain silent," says Master Eckhart. And Pascal remarks that every trouble stems from the fact that people are not capable of remaining alone in a room.

These statements do not belong only to our times, in which a feverish state permeates every field of life. Anxiousness, inner conflict, and lack of peace are elements that pertain to our human condition. Even in the preceding ages courage was needed to retreat so as to temporarily wait for God, in quiet and in silence. The words of Carl Friedrich von Weizsäcker: "I could not live without constantly returning to silence," show us the aim of John of the Cross. For him, to pray deep inside one's heart and be united to God start where one renounces to act on personal initiative, letting go of one's own reasoning and, by keeping silence, allowing oneself to be carried away by God. What is said today about meditation comes close to what John of the Cross defines as being empty for God, as loving attention, as touching God. In the sixteenth century, the word meditation meant conversational reflection, to think.

"Some insist they should proceed forward through meditation or reflection. By doing so, they rely too much on their own strength, and this is a mistake since, during the dark night of the soul, God leads the soul along a path that is completely different—the path of contemplation. The former is the way of reflection that resorts to the mind whereas the latter has nothing to do with meditation and reflection. Our heart must be maintained in total quiet, even if we may be convinced that we are wasting time. In that circumstance, the only thing we can do is to clear our spirit of perceptions and thoughts, meditations and considerations, and to abandon ourselves exclusively to a peaceful and loving attention to God."[11]

The active night in which the person who prays endeavors on one's own to attain tranquillity, freedom, and quiet, is what is known as the night of the spirit, the night in which the light of God is perceived by the soul as darkness. In fact, at this stage the soul perceives but is still not transformed. John of the Cross wishes those who pray to be alert and awake for the night of the spirit.

To describe how to be open before God, he uses common terms such as relaxing, doing nothing, freeing oneself, being at peace. Today, people pay a lot of attention to these values because they have experienced that faith in God and confidence in the message of salvation brought by Jesus remain abstract until the one who searches for God is taken for what he is. Karl Rahner adds: God has created man as a being who can still live without having faith in someone or something. This is why we can actually open ourselves in faith to Jesus Christ. God does not act against nature.

"These spiritual directors, not understanding souls that tread the path of quiet and solitary contemplation, since they themselves have not reached it and do not know what it is to part with discursive meditation, think these souls are idle.... These directors do not know what spirit is. They do a great injury to God and show disrespect toward Him by intruding with a rough hand where He is working. It cost God a great deal to bring these souls to this stage... so that He might speak to their hearts, which is what He always desires. Since He it is Who now reigns in the soul with an abundance of peace and calm, He takes the initiative Himself."[12]

Spiritual advisers do more through their life than through their advice. Before teaching the others how to pray they themselves should experience God's peace. For John of the Cross, being with God in tranquility is true love, since love has time to spare for others. "Nothing is better and more necessary than love. A little amount of pure love is more precious to God and of more advantage to the Church than all works put together.... Extremely active people should consider they would be more useful to the Church and much more acceptable to God—not to mention the good example they would set—if they spent in prayer only half the time they dedicate to work. Good works can only be done in virtue of God."[13]

IV. Not doing

John of the Cross and Teresa of Avila were reproached by those who believe silent meditation and inner prayer with no visible action are a waste of time, a state of idleness dangerous to the life of faith. Even today, similar objections are raised. Some extremely active Christians are displeased by the fact that at times there are silent pauses during liturgical services or common prayer; that is, when just for once they have to make a pause in their flow of words to God.

After an exercise focused on keeping silence, the participants exchanged their experiences. A woman said: "I did not know what I was supposed to do in all that silence, so I quickly prayed the Rosary." This statement symbolizes the mood of many Christians who are accustomed to formulate ready-made prayers, but who deep down do not know how to deal personally with God. Five or ten minutes of silence suffice to make them experience anguish or discomfort. Still, this does not intend to pass judgment on the way these people pray. Teresa of Avila used to say that we can also attain the deepest contemplation through vocal prayer. Still, this is a symptom of how very seldom personal prayer is practiced and of how often it is seen as a duty and a sacrifice.

"As instinctive human beings we are always dissatisfied and in a bad mood like hungry people. But what is this hunger that no creature can satisfy, compared to the fulfillment granted by the spirit of God? This uncreated fulfillment cannot penetrate our heart unless the created hunger of lust is first driven away from it."[14] According to John of the Cross, by being silent and becoming still before God, we are transformed from surly and selfish individuals into peaceful and generous persons. Doing nothing for some time and expecting everything from God does not mean, according to John, to let ourselves be carried away aimlessly, but to wake up to our inner reality which only God can satisfy. The lack of satisfaction experienced in prayer is heightened by the desire of "doing" something, which renders the individual spiritually deaf. "The more habituated he becomes to this calm, the deeper his experience of the general, loving knowledge of God will grow. This knowledge is more enjoyable than all other things, because without the soul's labor it affords peace, rest, savor, and delight."[15]

According to John of the Cross, the discovery of God implies a process, not the fossilization of one who prays. The saint does not disapprove of our meditating on the Passion and Resurrection of Christ. He wishes us to go further, however, telling us not to stop halfway, since even the most beautiful painting of God is not God but our own idea of God. The praying person "should not interfere with forms of discursive meditations and imaginings. Otherwise his soul will be disquieted and drawn out of its peaceful contentment to distaste and repugnance. And if, as we said, scruples about his inactivity arise, he should remember that pacification of soul (making it calm and peaceful, inactive and desireless) is no small accomplishment."[16]

V. Being empty

John of the Cross refers to the existence of an inner space of emptiness, to our being free from every linkage with things. He urges those who pray to abandon their doubts as to whether their inactivity is right or wrong; the essential thing being that they keep their minds free from any "noisy" thoughts. "The light is never lacking to the soul, but because of creature forms and veils weighing upon and covering it, the light is never infused. If a person will eliminate these impediments and veils, and live in pure nakedness and poverty of spirit, as we shall explain later, his soul in its simplicity and purity will then be immediately transformed into simple and pure Wisdom, the Son of God. As soon as natural things are driven out of the enamored soul, the divine are naturally and supernaturally infused since there can be no void in nature."[17]

The experience of inner and external stripping is not a goal in itself. God loves his creation and all it contains. To be deprived of things does not imply abandoning them because they are evil or because they could become obstacles to our growth. Privations and emptiness help us to give each thing the importance it should have. Thus, we do not long for them but just let them be. The person who is interiorly stripped is the poor person to whom nothing belongs but to whom everything is given because the spirit of God can thus find its way and penetrate a purified heart.

Even the feelings of peace and joy which are so important for John of the Cross are subject to the law of emptiness. There is no actual assurance in this life. "Some people feel a strong experience of God's closeness. This feeling, however, has not yet anything to do with the essence of God. God remains concealed to the human being, and because he is hidden, the person must search for him. However profound this experience may be it will not bring us to a closer union with God. If we have to deal with darkness, aridity, and discomfort, we should not think that God is farther away than before."[18] Here lies the basic teaching on the active and passive night of the soul. It is not in our power to experience peace or discomfort, light or darkness, in meditation. The subjective experience depends on multiple factors: also Teresa of Avila says that the person who has entered the inner dwelling of the soul's castle, does not always find peace and joy, even if he or she returns there continuously.

Our human condition is temporary. "Until we do not attain what we love, we are similar to an empty glass that waits to be filled, like a hungry person who is avid for food, like a sick person who moans to be cured, like someone who is suspended in the air and whose feet cannot touch the ground. This is the experience of those who are imbued by love for God.... Love for God is the health of the soul.

84

And our soul will be diseased as long as this love is not perfect."[19]

Who of us can say that our love and prayer are perfect? John of the Cross is objective. The more we are aware of God's closeness in our contemplative prayer, the happier and quieter we become. Still, we shall always be, until the end, poor and hungry creatures, sick people who have only God to turn to.

VI. Not seeing

"The dark night penetrates the innermost depth of the person, establishing order among his or her passions. It strengthens and purifies a person's inclination toward God, eliminating or diminishing those that belong to the senses."[20] "Regarding the dark night, David says: 'In an uninhabited, waterless, sterile, and pathless land I appeared before you to learn about your virtues and your glory' (Ps 62: 2-3). From the aridity or emptiness of the night, our soul draws humility of spirit.... From here stems the true love of our neighbor, because now we value the latter without passing judgments as we used to do in the past, when we saw only ourselves, not the others, as people filled with zeal. Now we only see our own misery."[21]

John of the Cross always deals with our faith in Jesus Christ, with entering the glory of God. For him, to believe implies an unconditional trust in a superior being. Faith is experienced as love, where not wanting to see is taken seriously. "A man who is not yet entirely blind will not allow a good guide to lead him. Still able to perceive a little, he thinks that road he sees is the best, for he is unable to see other and better ones."[22] Thus, John of the Cross urges us to make a radical decision which opens up a completely new way to our consideration of God and his gifts.

Life implies a risk. It is similar to a journey in which we must be always prepared for something new. There is no time to build ourselves a nest along the way, to get lost while picking flowers. The road along the dark night of the soul is hard; still, it is sweet for those who know that their blindness will lead them to unexpected horizons. "In order to visit unknown lands, the wayfarer travels along unfamiliar roads and proceeds, uncertain and doubtful, without counting upon his own experience but on the guidance of others. He could not visit new regions if he wouldn't walk totally new ways, leaving familiar ones behind."[23]

To engage in a life of meditation is to start a bold and energetic journey based on the experience gained by others. It does not mean to draw away from the world and its beauty but rather to draw closer to it from a deeper dimension, thus contributing to its transformation and transfiguration. "In the dark night [of the soul] God acts in the innermost region of the soul through his plentiful grace. At this stage our soul is purified of its ignorance and everyday faults.... The dark night of the soul obscures everything. It humbles the spirit and makes it miserable but only to exhort and raise it; it impoverishes and empties it of every possession and earthly affection but only so that it may expand divinely and enjoy all heavenly things...."[24]

All people, even those religiously oriented, tend to stability, to habit, to establishing a linkage with tradition. This can be something wholesome in many aspects, but ultimately this should not be a stumbling block to spiritual freedom developed through meditation. "This is the interpretation we should give to Christ's reply to the query of the Samaritan woman about the place best suited for prayer—the temple or the mountain. His answer was that true prayer is annexed neither to the temple nor to the mountain, but that the adorers who please the Father are those who adore Him in spirit and truth. [Jn 4:20-24]"[25]

Not seeing also includes not understanding. Meditation in the obscurity of trust implies acknowledging that there is someone else who knows our path better than we ourselves do. "The soul must go to God by not comprehending rather than comprehending, and it must exchange the mutable and comprehensible for the Immutable and Incomprehensible."[26] The incomprehensible, the transcendental lies beyond our experience and it is a gift. "Entering on the road means leaving one's own road, or better, moving on to the goal; and turning from one's own mode implies entry into what has no mode, that is, God. A person who reaches this state no longer has any modes or methods, still less is he—nor can he be—attached to them. I am referring to modes of understanding, taste, and feeling. Within himself, though, he possesses all methods, like one who though having nothing yet possesses all things."[27]

VII. Believing

For John of the Cross, maturity is attained by those who meditate and immerse themselves in God and in their own nothingness. For the spirit who longs to know, believing implies an unconditional surrender, the entry into someone who transcends us infinitely and to whose action we abandon ourselves. "As for God, who will stop Him from accomplishing His desires in the soul that is resigned, annihilated, and despoiled? Insofar as he is capable, a person must void himself of all, so that, however many supernatural communications he receives, he will continually live as though denuded of them and in darkness. Like a blind man he must lean on dark faith, accept it for his guide and light, and rest on nothing of what he understands, tastes, feels, or imagines. All these perceptions are a darkness that will lead him astray. Faith lies beyond all this understanding, taste, feeling, and imagining."[28]

What the actual center of the person is, the center Teresa of Avila and John of the Cross are searching for together, is experienced in faith in a most profound way. "Desire to enter for Christ into complete nudity, emptiness, and poverty in everything in the world. In this nakedness the spirit finds its quietude and rest. For in coveting nothing, nothing raises it up and nothing weighs it down, because it is in the center of its humility. When it covets something in this very desire it is wearied."[29]

Those who not only know but also experience who they are and who God is, those who are carried, guided, emptied of their own imaginations and desires, are at rest in themselves and are humble, which means that they rest in truth. This inner experience is their consolation, their identity, their knowing they are in Christ, who is their model and assistance.

"For anyone fortunate enough to possess the ability to journey in the obscurity of faith, as a blind man with his guide, and depart from all natural phantasms and intellectual reasonings, walks securely."[30] John of the Cross teaches a theology of inner emptiness, "for love of Christ." The descent of Christ into darkness and lack of understanding is continued in those who believe, hope, and love. Emptiness, abandoning one's own behavior, becoming quiet and silent lead those who meditate to obscurity, but an obscurity filled with comfort because only now a person reaches one's true center, finding oneself close to transcendence.

Faith is an abyss which projects us outside of ourselves into new glory, even though it is still hidden. John of the Cross never tires of repeating: "The more importance given to any clear and distinct apprehension, natural or supernatural, the less capacity and preparedness the soul has for entering the abyss of faith where all else is absorbed. As we pointed out, none of the supernatural forms and ideas that can be had by the memory is God, and the soul must empty itself of all that is not God in order to go to God... for in relation to God, the more a soul hopes the more it attains. And when, precisely, it is more dispossessed of things, it hopes more."[31]

Who nothing possesses, hopes to attain everything. Only God can satisfy the totality of a position such as that adopted by Saint John of the Cross. All that we try, touch, know, and can calculate is not God. To meditate means to come face to face with the absence of every imagination in order to be close to God. This nothingness becomes superabundance in Christ. The world, as God has created it with its multiplicity, has been brought into the Resurrection of Christ and transformed through faith.

VIII. Loving

For John of the Cross, passive theology, a concept he frequently uses, culminates in a theology of personal love. The experiences of obscurity or consolation, darkness or light, have the characteristics of a personal call for those who love.

The experience of suffering belongs to this sphere. In John's view the painfulness of our existence is not cancelled but rather lived in faith and hope. Suffering is an element of transformation. It is something so precious that Christ himself, the beloved Son of God, was not afraid to take it upon himself, not because he loved to suffer, but because he wished to redeem us on the strength of this extreme self-giving. "The person walks assuredly in the dark because he or she walks through suffering. The path of suffering is more secure and fruitful than that of pleasure and action. In suffering we experience the strength of God, while in action alone, we rely too much on ourselves and become weak. In suffering we are purified and thus become wise and prudent."[32]

The ability to accept and bear suffering is a sign of the honesty of a love acknowledged among those who follow the crucified and risen Christ. One of the sufferings of human existence is that even in all the consolations granted in prayer, God still remains hidden.

It is important that people educate themselves to peace and silence. Even Isaiah used to say: "By waiting and by calm you shall be saved, in quiet and in trust your strength lies" (Is 30:15), and John of the Cross encourages us: "Rejoice and exult in your inner peace, because you are extremely close to God. Love and adore him here. Do not search him outside yourself for you would only get distracted and tired. He cannot be found more surely, more quickly and more closely, and cannot be enjoyed more profoundly than within yourself. You should reflect on the fact that he dwells in you, even though he appears hidden from you. It is something enormous to know the dwelling of him who is hidden in order to look for him there with certainty."[33]

In all situations God is close to those who search and who love. Since he takes people seriously, those who engage in meditation receive, on the one hand, peace and consolation and thank God for this participation. But they also put up with the dark, with what is incomprehensible and difficult, keeping the image of Jesus crucified before them. For those who love, the wound of one is the wound of the other. Feelings are mutual. God does not give himself completely to the person for him or her to become rich in knowledge of God, but for love.... True and unchangeable love cannot conceal anything from those who love. In fact, God reveals to people the secrets of the

Incarnation and the way they must follow to attain their Redemption."[34]

The silence of spending time with God in meditation makes us understand God's redeeming work better than meditating upon this mystery for a very long time. "How unique the longing of lovers who prefer to enjoy being alone rather than in the company of others. In fact, even though they are together, the presence of a stranger can be enough for them to lose their ease.... The reason is that love is the union of two persons."[35] The teachings of John of the Cross about contemplation recall an experience of identity of human and divine love, without cancelling the sensible difference. John of the Cross applies what is a characteristic sign of the personal union between two beings to his experience with Christ and God. Solitude, silence, forgetfulness are necessary elements that stem from love. "And the Samaritan woman forgot the water and the water pot because of the sweetness of God's words."[36]

But the Samaritan woman did not leave things as they were. In fact, she took a second step by hurrying to announce God's new message to her friends. The transformation of lovers is so great that the duality is no longer perceived, even though it continues to exist. " 'Those who are moved by the Spirit of God are sons of God Himself' (Rom 8:14). Accordingly, the intellect of this soul is God's intellect; its will is God's will; its memory is the memory of God; and its delight is God's delight; and although the substance of this soul is not the substance of God, since it cannot undergo a substantial conversion into Him, it has become God through participation in God, being united to and absorbed in Him, as it is in this state.... Consequently the soul is dead to all that it was in itself, which was death to it, and alive to what God is in Himself."[37]

Meditation, exercising ourselves in keeping silence, vigilance in keeping God's word in us, carry in themselves elements of death: renunciation, privation, emptiness and detachment from creatures. However, this death is not final, nor is our daily experience of suffering, sickness, and weakness. For those who meditate, all these are transformed into glory of God. "[God] is the cause to it all. And in that awakening, which is as though one were to awaken and breathe, the soul feels a strange delight.... I do not desire to speak of this spiration, filled for the soul with good and glory and delicate love of God, for I am aware of being incapable of so doing, and were I to try, it might seem less than it is.... He breathes the Holy Spirit in it... absorbing it most profoundly.... Since the breathing is filled with good and glory, the Holy Spirit, through this breathing, filled the soul with good and glory, in which He enkindled it in love of Himself, indescribably and incomprehensibly, in the depths of God."[38]

III. THERESE OF LISIEUX

ECSTASY OF THE HEART

Those who still believe that the "little way" maintained by Thérèse of Lisieux is only right for "minors," lacking the height, width, and depth of other ways, change their mind when they discover in Thérèse's life and writings that her teachings drew their nourishment from the power of meditation. Thérèse was a meditative person. What today has to be gained with great effort by undertaking new ways of meditation and methods borrowed from the East, was bestowed upon Thérèse as a gift, due to her predisposition and the presence of favorable circumstances. Thanks to her meditative capacity she was able to cope with and defeat the hardships encountered throughout her short life. Precisely to people of our times can Thérèse explain the meaning of meditation and the place it must occupy in a person's life. Therefore, Thérèse's gift can become our own.

Since her childhood, Thérèse was immersed in the beauty and grandeur of nature: "I still feel," she writes, "the profound and *poetic* impressions which were born in my soul at the sight of fields enamelled with *corn-flowers* and

95

all types of wild flowers. Already I was in love with the *wide-open spaces*. Space and the gigantic fir trees, the branches sweeping down to the ground, left in my heart an impression similar to the one I experience still today at the sight of nature."[1] In this passage we find an indication of what true and spontaneous meditation is all about. By being completely open to what surrounds us, when we meditate we allow the other being to enter our existence. In the encounter with faraway horizons, space, trees, flowers, and colors, the contemplative soul expands and welcomes the dimensions of the one it encounters. The soul perceives a response deep inside, the birth of feelings that embrace everything in its entirety and that allows the soul to take possession of everything. Everything is permeable, both inner and outer things meet without pain. In this perception of nature, the person who meditates becomes capable of welcoming deep inside the heart what is directed towards it from among human and divine things (Rilke).

The early death of her mother conferred to Thérèse's meditative skill the capacity of identifying herself with a new dimension: that of suffering, of not being able to understand. About her mother's death, Thérèse tells us that she did not "speak to anyone about the feelings I experienced. I looked and listened in silence." The four-year-old child stayed for a long time in front of the coffin's lid: "Though I'd never seen one before, I understood what it was."[2] Thérèse watched and listened, both in joy and torment, and was struck dumb in awe and outrage. However, deep inside her heart Thérèse understood. In meditation, impressions are not suppressed but accepted for what they are, either as positive or negative experiences.

The child's suffering persisted and for the moment could not be alleviated. Thérèse had to endure this new experience no matter what toll it could have taken. The world from which her mother had departed became ever so dark. Despite its beauty, the earth was now a place of exile. Ever since her mother's death, Thérèse shifted her meditation from nature onto God, grace, the life beyond, where one searches for what one has lost or longs for. Thérèse's ability to extend her meditation to life beyond death was a beneficial counterweight to her imaginings and lack of human relationships.

Thérèse loved reading and observing paintings. In her eleventh year of life one of her instructors asked her how she spent those days in which there happened to be no school. "I told her I went behind my bed in an empty space which was there, and that it was easy to close myself in with my bed-curtain and that 'I *thought*.' 'But what do you think about?' she asked. 'I think about God, about life, about ETERNITY... I *think*'.... I understand now that I was making mental prayer without knowing it and that God was already instructing me in secret."[3]

Thérèse "pondered," but it was a pondering of the heart that stemmed from the consideration of love. To her, religion was not something constrictive, or something acquired by reading. For her, devotion to God meant speaking with one's heart, experiencing the inner and outer realities as one. Jesus Christ was not a concept, something to believe in, but a personal reality. The experience of his love urged her to establish a bond, to be decisive. Since Thérèse became aware of the impotence of human freedom, she decided to lose herself completely in the freedom of her divine partner. In her bond with Christ, in her desire to contemplate and to be contemplated, she recognized at the age of thirteen, "the immense void of the desires," which "cannot be filled by the praises of an instant"[4] "I felt," she writes, "it was more valuable to speak to God than to speak about Him."[5] For Thérèse, heaven meant "a real and eternal family reunion."[6] "All the great truths of religion, the mysteries of eternity, plunged my soul into a state of joy not of this earth. I experienced already what God reserved for those who love him... and seeing the eternal rewards had no proportion to life's small sacrifices."[7]

Due to her persistence, Thérèse was allowed at age fifteen to enter the Carmelite order, a cloister of strict observance, but first enjoyed her contact with art and nature on her trip to Rome. In 1886 Thérèse was cured from the scruples that stemmed from her acute sensitivity and religious torments, and since then she does not show any inhibition or morbosity. Regarding her trip through Switzerland, she writes: "How much good these beauties of nature, poured out *in such profusion*, did my soul.... I hadn't eyes enough to take in everything. Standing by the window I almost lost my breath; I would have liked to be on both sides of the car.... When I saw all these beauties, very profound thoughts came to life in my soul.... The religious life appeared to me *exactly as it is* with its *subjections*, its small sacrifices carried out in the shadows. I understood how easy it is to become all wrapped up in self, forgetting entirely the sublime goal of one's calling. I said to myself: When I am a prisoner in Carmel and trials come my way and I have only a tiny bit of the starry heavens to contemplate, I shall remember what my eyes have seen today. This thought will encourage me and I shall easily forget my own little interests, recalling the grandeur and power of God, this God whom I want to love alone. I shall not have the misfortune of snatching after *straws.*"[8]

Thérèse understood the reality of human existence. Her devotion to something superior in meditation was the prelude to her devotion towards the Supreme Being—God. Still, the beauty and majesty of nature are in conflict with the everyday life of society. Like Pascal, Thérèse saw people outstretched between everything and nothing, between misery and greatness. From the existential experiences drawn from her meditations on nature, she oriented herself towards that which she recognized as divine. Everything in her thirsted for greatness and immensity—but the exhausting warfare of everyday life had to be defeated.

Thérèse also admired humanity's accomplishments in the arts and sciences. However, human power and greatness did not satisfy her. She wished to participate in the power of God himself, whose love is directed to both the greatest and the smallest of creatures. In Jesus Christ, God had accepted not only humanity's *gifts* but also its misery, its inclination towards sin and its capacity for abusing its freedom. Thérèse believed that this divine acceptance of the human being who is a sinner, and who rejects divine mercy, is greater than all the beauties in the world. It shows passionate love for humanity on the part of God who lets himself be crucified and destroyed to allow the lost creature share again in his glory. For Thérèse the greatness of the crucified Love constituted the subject matter of her meditation in Carmel.

At the age of sixteen she devised a schedule she would

follow until her death. We read in her letters: "Life is a treasure, every instant is an eternity.... To see God face to face, to be one thing only with him! Only Jesus *is*, all the rest *is not*.... Therefore, let us love him to the point of craziness. Our mission is to forget ourselves, to destroy ourselves.... We are of such little account, and still Jesus wants our sacrifices and love to be instrumental in the salvation of souls."[9]

Thérèse's meditation became contemplation that brought *passio* and *actio* together. The active and passive night of the soul, as John of the Cross calls this state, purified her actions from egocentrism and dangerous independence. For Thérèse, this inner night meant not only suffering but also joy which stemmed from the fact that her actions were guided by love. The more Thérèse suffered, the more active she became: "I have understood it pretty well, we do not find happiness in the objects surrounding us, but rather deep inside our soul. We can find happiness in a prison as perfectly as in a palace; proof of it is the fact that I am happier in Carmel, even among inner and external trials, than in the world, surrounded by the comforts of life and especially by the sweetness of my family life!"[10]

Through the joy of identifying herself with Jesus crucified, Thérèse's prayer was extremely simple. For her, the word *love* included everything to which meditation and prayer aspire, all that contemplation bestows. Love was the simplest formula of her life oriented to the gospel. Thérèse provided modest advice which was, however, effective for prayer: "It is good to recollect oneself frequently and guide one's intentions without, however, forcing the spirit. God knows the beautiful thoughts and sensible intentions we would like to have."[11]

"I say very simply to God what I wish to say, without composing beautiful sentences, and He always understands me. For me, *prayer* is an aspiration of the heart, it is a simple glance directed to heaven, it is a cry of gratitude and love in the midst of trial as well as joy; finally, it is something great, supernatural, which expands my soul and unites me to Jesus."[12]

Thérèse lacked the teachers who would have explained to her the writings or doctrines of Carmel, but she herself became a teacher without knowing it. With the help of grace and her personal search, she found what was right for her and for others. Although she was not familiar with modern concepts such as conversion of the heart, and innermost dimension, she was able to penetrate the depth of her heart, the innermost region of her soul, the experience which helps the human person to be oneself, and which opens the way to both God and neighbor.

IV. EDITH STEIN

1. STRICKEN BY GOD

Don't we often hear, even in a Christian environment, that we are no longer capable of having a real and proper experience of God, of experiencing transcendence? Moreover, philosophy, theology, and psychology readily maintain that these experiences are only a myth. According to Josef Ratzinger, however, these judgments are reckless and can be easily refuted by the reliable testimonies of many men and women.

Edith Stein's life offers a model of how even we who live in the twentieth century, in the midst of such debate and confusion, are capable of experiencing the One who made our heart restless so that it would find rest in him (Saint Augustine). The different phases of Edith Stein's spiritual evolution are of interest to those who are in search of God today. She was a Jew, atheist, student, Red Cross volunteer, philosopher, convert, teacher, scholar and feminist, higher education teacher, and finally Carmelite and martyr for her people in a gas chamber in Auschwitz. This is the life of a human being who did not escape from our contemporary problems, a person who was open to the demands and needs of our society, who complied entirely with her duty and who searched the way to achieve a more human and meaningful future. If we could ask Edith Stein on what behavioral foundation she developed this rich program of life until her death, she would certainly tell us first about her obstinate search for truth and the meaning of life. As a young woman she refused to believe in a transcendental God, and much less did she have an experience of him. Still, she tried to be honest, unselfish and concerned for others. She was honest, because she detested to say or do anything untrue in order to draw some profit. She defined herself an atheist because to her, the God of her Jewish faith did not exist. She was selfless and socially concerned, and as a scholar and student she endeavored to serve others, being always cordial and helpful. Esteemed for her stable personality, her family and friends soon asked for her advice on various matters.

Still, there was something essential lacking this young student. She was shy, although self-confident. She was gentle, ready to help, and was used to being esteemed because she had something to give. Yet, she felt alone and longed to find a meaning for her life. She discovered this void in a disquieting way while studying psychology in Breslau (1911). The psychology of those days was described as a "soulless psychology," which left it up to each individual to imagine, beyond the perception of the senses, a spiritual unity, a meaning, a soul. In her longing, Edith Stein came across the writings of the illustrious Jewish philosopher Edmund Husserl, who was endeavoring to rediscover the existence of the spirit. Husserl was

103

investigating the deep knowledge of the essence, the being of things. Thus, he taught his disciples respect for objective values, not to have prejudice in reflecting the phenomenon of human existence. Edith Stein hoped to find in Husserl's method an answer to her questions and moved to the University of Göttingen. Thus, she became one of the teacher's most faithful students, but she learned that after all not even Husserl could provide her with an answer to her question about truth. As with any human reality, Husserl's philosophy, even though practiced by its follower in a rigorously scientific manner, was limited and subject to error. Edith Stein herself was more radical than Husserl. She did not want to dwell in subjectivity, limiting herself to the kingdom of ideas, but wanted to deal earnestly and be objective.

Two encounters at Göttingen led Edith Stein to the threshold of a new world—the world of faith. Max Scheler, a Jew who converted to Christianity in 1913, held lectures on the beauty of the Catholic faith. For the first time in her life, Edith Stein ran into concepts such as sanctity, humility, and purity. She admitted that all this was unknown to her, but she faced these new realities objectively and as a learner. She had not yet opened herself to the world of faith but she discovered that there were values which she could not blindly neglect. She was however led beyond the threshold of faith by a second encounter, this time with Adolf Reinach, Husserl's disciple. This philosopher, an Evangelical convert who has left an indelible memory in his environment, led Edith Stein to an experience that transcended the frontiers of natural reason. In regard to this, she said: "I was overjoyed by this first encounter [with

Reinach] and full of deep gratitude. It was the first time a person approached me with such a pure kindness of heart. It seems obvious that one's closest relatives and friends would show such love. But there was something I could perceive in him that was completely different: it was like discovering an entirely different world for the first time."[1]

It was probably then that Edith Stein experienced God for the first time. God manifested himself to her through an individual's love and kindness, as Someone totally different but still very close to her. Her outlook on the new world deepened through this experience, which was a confirmation to her that God's life can be communicated, and how this had been done in the Passion and Resurrection of Christ.

In 1917, Reinach died in Flandern. Edith Stein, like his other friends, was deeply moved and especially concerned about his young widow. When asked, Edith immediately agreed to organize the posthumous works of Reinach, who had fallen in the war. Still, she dreaded her encounter with Mrs. Reinach. She did not know what to say to give her comfort, since Edith did not believe in an eternal life. She went to Mrs. Reinach in distress and thought the latter would show the same feeling. To her great surprise, however, the widow did not look shattered. On the contrary, despite the hard trial she was going through, because of her Christian faith, she had the strength to console the unbelieving and doubtful Edith. This experience struck Edith Stein. Confronted with the sight of this woman who was full of hope, her rationalistic prejudices crumbled, and she understood that what changes a person is not scientific knowledge but truth itself.

This experience of God was so deeply recorded in her memory, that shortly before her death she could still say: "This was my first encounter with the cross and with the power of God it transmits to its carriers. For the first time I saw before me the Church, born from the sufferings of the Redeemer, from his victory over the sting of death. It was then that my unbelief was shattered and Christ shone in the mystery of the cross."[2]

Now a violent struggle began in Edith Stein's life. God himself had touched the depths of her unbelief; this was such a vital and immediate experience that reason could no longer question it. Still, a human being is made not only of reason, but of will as well, and the will has the power to reject whatever the reason suggests.

Edith Stein expressed the mystery of our will's freedom in these words: "It is the religious experience that will make a convinced atheist aware of God's existence. He cannot shun faith and live at its same level; he does not allow faith to start acting on him but remains firmly anchored to his scientific view of the world which faith could completely shatter."[3] With psychological sharpness she thus describes a common disposition of the soul, which we so often find in ourselves as well. We don't surrender to the consequences that derive from our experiences in relation to God. We act as though they did not exist and try to cover them up with something superficial.

From 1917 to 1921 Edith Stein lived in this conflict which she compared to a "death shadow." She started reading the New Testament asking herself whether she should join the Evangelical or the Catholic Church. However, her will remained paralyzed until something unexpected happened.

During a visit to a friend of hers called Hedwig Conrad-Martius, she came across the autobiography of Saint Teresa of Avila, which her friend kept in the library. Staying up throughout the night she read the whole book without taking a breath and after closing it said: "This is the truth."

Edith Stein saw her own struggle, needs, and questions reflected in the work of this great Spaniard. Teresa of Avila, proclaimed Doctor of the Church in 1970 by Pope Paul VI, proved to Edith Stein that we cannot be faithful to God or to ourselves unless we respond to the experience of God. God does not call us so that we sleep, but in order that, as beings capable of responding, we become vigilant and do something concrete. For Teresa of Avila, to believe did not mean just believing in the existence of God and the dogmas proposed by our faith, but it meant having a personal relationship with God. She tirelessly exhorted everyone to make the exercise to converse with God and Jesus Christ. For her, to pray did not mean to recite words by heart, but it was an experience of friendship and love between God and the person.

Teresa of Avila bestowed new energy upon Edith Stein, who felt deeply understood. On January 1, 1922, Edith Stein was baptized and her only wish was to enter the Teresian Carmel. Still, her friends did not understand her experience of God. They were astonished to see her pray hours in the churches of Speyer or Beuron and believed she was overdoing it. Consequently, they urged her to put her talent at the service of her fellow human beings and not to vanish behind the walls of a cloister. Some priests advised her to do the same thing. Edith Stein kept silent and obeyed, also because her mother, an observant Jew, would not have endured two similar blows all at once—Edith's conversion and her admission to the convent.

Throughout ten years of hard work as an educator, a translator of Saint Thomas Aquinas, and an upholder of feminine rights, Edith Stein learned what it meant to adhere to the experience of God and at the same time to feel excluded from real professional aspirations. She was relatively silent about what she learned from God, but she admitted that she felt "changed" since her conversion. She unconsciously chose an expression used by the mystics. Paul, Augustine, Teresa of Avila, Thérèse of Lisieux, Charles de Foucauld, and others describe their experience of God in similar words. Indirectly, from her letters and writings, we can understand how intensely Edith Stein lived her friendship with God, how much this was a two-way relationship of giving and receiving. Friends and students noticed her influence, her self-denial, her taking Christ's message with utter seriousness. In one of her lectures she said: "There is a big difference between the self-sufficient life of a good Catholic who fulfills his own duties, reads a good newspaper, makes the right choices but, for the rest, does what pleases him, and a life led according to the dictates of God, in the simplicity of a child and the humility of the publican. But those who cross this border, shall never turn backwards."[4]

Edith had the innocence of a child and the humility of a publican, but this did not make her childish or inexperienced concerning the world. She was an entirely committed and active woman and through school reformation programs she attempted to create new avenues for women's education, to include women in modern society.

In 1933, the national-socialists indeliberately helped Edith Stein to reach her life's goal. Due to the racist laws in force, she was prevented from teaching at the Pedagogy Institute of Münster, and in the fall of 1933 Edith entered the Carmel in Cologne. More than once she could have escaped abroad, but she preferred to stay behind with her suffering Jewish people. She often spoke to her visitors about the inner peace she had found in Carmel.

Edith Stein was a good companion to her sisters in the cloister. The joy of her encounter with God made her capable of sharing the suffering brought about by her people's fate without becoming bitter. She knew that as long as she stayed in the convent, her life was in danger. That explains why in Carmel she chose to be called Teresia Benedicta a Cruce (blessed by the cross). She had experienced the strength the cross bestows upon those who carry it out of love for Christ. The darker it became around her the more secure she felt in the light of God.

After the assault against the Jews during the *Kristallnacht* in 1938, Edith decided not to hold the Carmel of Cologne in jeopardy any longer and promptly accepted her transfer to the Carmel in Echt, Holland. It was there, after her philosophical-theological treatise *Finite Being and Eternal Being*, written in Cologne, that Edith wrote an analysis of the mystical doctrine of John of the Cross, father of her order. She writes: "The nuptial union between God and the soul is the purpose for which it has been created. This is obtained through the cross, fulfilled on the cross and sealed with the cross for all eternity."[5] This was not a figure of speech. Edith Stein lived each of her words until the point of the crucifixion of her own soul and body.

We know how she went to her death. Calm and resigned, after being arrested at Echt, she grasped Sister Rose's hand and in the presence of the SS-thugs said: "Come on, let's die for our people."[6]

Edith Stein faced her arrest with all the love of a heart offered in immolation. At the concentration camp in Westerbork she forgot about herself and looked after the other prisoners, helping and consoling them. Later, a member of the staff in Westerbork said that talking with her in the middle of that horrible predicament had been like "a trip to another world."[7]

On August 9, 1942, Edith Stein died in the gas chamber alongside her Jewish brothers and sisters. From this annihilation a light broke out, illuminating all those who would wish to see it. Through her life, Edith Stein says to us: "God is here, living among us, and his presence is felt even in the midst of disaster."

2. SUGGESTIONS FOR MEDITATION

For many years Edith Stein could not enter Carmel, which would have offered her room for reflection and meditation. However, as a woman committed to her field of work, she tried to create for herself pauses she considered necessary during her productive working day. In a letter addressed to working women she offered some suggestions on how to attain inner silence. She writes:

"We can and must place our soul in God's hands. We must be ready to receive him and let our souls be shaped by him. This means, first of all, to become empty and silent. By nature our soul is filled with so many things, that one thought always draws another, maintaining our soul in continuous movement, often in turmoil and revolt. If our daily duties and preoccupations have not already disturbed our night's sleep, they crowd around us as soon as we wake up in the morning. We are anxious because we do not know how we shall be able to fulfill our numerous daily tasks. And we are not sure of the way to do them. We are tempted to get up and run away as if we were being hunted. At this stage we need to pull ourselves together, to quiet our hearts and tell ourselves: 'Nothing should disturb our peace. The first hour of the day belongs to the Lord.' "[1]

A human being does not live only on spontaneity. Every psychologist and pedagogue can show us that we assimilate impressions, fantasies, and knowledge when the same things or circumstances repeat themselves. This is especially true for our personal actions, for love, and for the maturing of our personality. Often, without realizing it, we carry out the same acts of devotion, trust, and mission on a daily basis. We often use a good word, a cordial smile, we console someone or struggle against our laziness, our anger, our stubbornness in always wanting to be right. Of course, all these exercises are not subject to definite time schedules. Since, however, we tend to do all or more than we can, it would be necessary, with a watch in our hand, to plan the moments for silent pauses in our working day. Tiredness often keeps us far from being silent. We would rather relieve ourselves by conversing with others. We should remember here that breathing and relaxation exercises are useful to condition our tired body and adopt an adequate listening position in relation to God.

Edith Stein clarified how much strength we can derive from the celebration of the Eucharist, how this makes us intimately capable and free, empty of ourselves and of our preoccupations. Silence and joy, which are given to us in our encounter with God, show us that we cannot act on our strength alone, but that it is God who sustains us.

Edith Stein describes the work of a teacher or an employee: "Now your working day starts. You may have to teach four or five consecutive lessons. This means you have to deal with a different subject every hour. However, there are times you cannot attain what you would like due to your tiredness, the unexpected interruptions, the insufficiency of the students, unpleasant, irritating, preoccupying circumstances. Or if you work in an office, you have to put up with unpleasant relationships with your superiors and co-workers, unfeasible demands, unjust reproaches, human meanness, maybe even the most varied types of faults. In the afternoon, you are likely to arrive home exhausted, where new setbacks may be waiting for you. Where has that morning freshness of the soul gone? Once more, you are tempted by the feeling of anger, revolt, resentment, remorse. And there are still a thousand things you have to do by evening! Should you continue your activity? Absolutely not, not unless silence has intervened, at least for a moment.

"Everybody should know or learn to know oneself in order to know where and how to find peace. The best thing to do, whenever possible, is to spend a few moments in front of the tabernacle, which sets us free from all our preoccupations. Whoever is unable to do this, because they need to stay home and get some physical rest, should find a pause to take a deep breath in their own room. And if there is no chance of withdrawing to find peace, because our duties prevent us from spending an hour in silence, then at least it is convenient to retreat internally for a moment, isolating ourselves from everyone, and finding refuge in the Lord. The Lord is certainly there; he can give us what we need at any time. Thus we shall continue the remainder of our daily activities. We may feel tired but we will have peace within ourselves. When night comes and we look back only to realize that our work has been done so imperfectly, and that what we had intended to do is still incomplete, when remorse and humiliation keep us wide awake, we should accept everything as it is and entrust it to God. In this way we shall be able to truly rest and start the following day as a new life."[2]

With this piece of advice Edith Stein shows us a method of meditation made for everybody. She stresses the importance of remaining empty and silent before God. To attain this, it is necessary to use violence to confront the external circumstances that oppress us, the duties that burden us, and our inner problems and insecurities. The liberating aspect offered to us by meditation lies in the fact that we let everything go for a while, and instead of directing our attention toward ourselves we direct it toward someone else who is before us.

Some people are psychologically aware of the purifying and liberating strength the exercise of silence bestows upon them, as well as the process of concentrating on not thinking, and on keeping silence. As Christians, we practice meditation, in silence, by becoming empty, mainly to purify our soul, which is certainly useful to better understand God, his will, and the meaning of our lives. Should this bring us inner freedom, flexibility, adaptability in the midst of torments, then we should welcome these fruits of meditation. It is important that in silence we learn to deal with people. A period of silence spent with others, in which we know we are in the presence of God and in God, often helps us to understand each other more than through a lot of praying.

It often happens that we are unable to say a single word to God; we only wish his closeness, we only want to be beside him. Peace pervades us and we feel reborn. We are given the strength to resist even in our darkest hours, when we no longer feel God's presence and perhaps we doubt his love and existence. Even in these temptations we should not give up our silent meditation. However, we should certainly not pray to obtain something from God but to give him something ourselves. The experience of inner peace prompts us to give ourselves to our neighbor and to take our own selves less seriously. It gives us the power to not dwell on our mistakes and our weaknesses nor at the way people treat us — whether with respect or contempt — and to forget ourselves, not because we do not attribute any value to all these things, but because in silence we learn where to find the true values of life.

At the beginning, the time we spend in solitude with God may be only a few minutes; later perhaps fifteen, or thirty. It will not be easy to make these pauses in our daily activity or work. But the more conscientiously we introduce them and the more strongly we allow our body and our breathing to take part in this silence, the more familiar this exercise will become for us.

Edith Stein stresses that each individual has to discover the way that is most suitable for him or her. "It is fundamental," she writes, "that each individual reflect, from time to time, how to organize his or her daily or annual schedule according to one's own inclinations and interpersonal relationships, in order to prepare the way for the Lord. Each individual will plan things differently and in the course of time will also have to be flexible and adaptable to the changing circumstances. However, the situation of each person's soul is different. The steps necessary to keep awake or rekindle one's linkage with eternity—contemplation, spiritual reading, participation in the liturgy and services—are not always equally fruitful for everyone at the same time. Meditation, for instance, cannot be practiced by everybody in the same way. It is important, from time to time, to use those things that are most effective."[3] Thus, Edith Stein shows that there can and should be different forms of prayer and meditation for different people.

Both, saints and spiritual masters, stress the fact that mystical life means to abandon oneself to the closeness of our living God. God is not the only one who acts, he takes our own actions into account. The person who is touched by him in faith makes a continuous effort to pray and to meditate, in order to become aware of his divine closeness. Our inner joy and identity as Christians depend on this awareness. Even suffering and difficulties do not become obstacles in this endeavor, but become paths to attain that personal, unmistakable experience of God.

NOTES

PART ONE: RELIGIOUS LIFE IN THE MIDST OF THE WORLD

I. INTRODUCTION

1. Cf. St. Teresa of Avila, *The Collected Works of* (Washington: ICS Publications, 1980), Vol. 2, 448.
2. Cf. K. Ware, *Schweigen im Gebet*. The meaning of "Hesychia" in "Erbe und Auftrag" (benedictine monthly magazine), 51 (1975), 6, 433.
3. Cf. E. Schillebeeckx, *Personale Begegnung mit Gott* (Mainz, 1964), 52.

II. WHAT IS MEDITATION?

1. Letter to Mater Petra OSU, April 1934, cited as in W. Herbstrith (Teresia A Matre Dei OCD), *Das wahre Gesicht Edith Steins* (Bergen-Enkheim, ²1973), 134.
2. A. de Saint-Exupéry, *Der Kleine Prinz* (Düsseldorf, 1971), 68.
3. A. Rosenberg, "Die Meditation des Schweigens" in R. Bleistein, H. G. Lubkoll, R. Pfützner (ed.) *Türen nach innen. Wege zur Meditation* (München), 113.
4. Cf. Avila, *Collected Works*, 319.

III. JESUS CHRIST: THE CENTER OF OUR MEDITATION

1. Kosho Uchiyama Roshi, *Weg zum Selbst. Zen-Wirklichkeit* (Weilheim, 1973), 41.

PART TWO: DISCOVERING THE LIVES
OF RELIGIOUS PEOPLE

I. TERESA OF AVILA

1. HER PERSONALITY

1. W. Herbstrith (Teresia a Matre Dei OCD), *Teresa von Avila. Meditation-Mystik-Mitmenschlichkeit* (Bergen-Enkheim, ³1974), 105.
2. Theresia von Jesu, "Gunstbezeigungen Gottes," # 13, in *Leben* (München-Kempten, 1960), 475.
3. Santa Teresa de Jesús, "Camino de Perfección" (Escorial-Manuscript), in *Obras Completas* (Madrid, 1967), 205, note 1, cited as in Herbstrith, 109-110.
4. Herbstrith, *Teresa von Avila*, 104.
5. Ibid., 104.
6. Ibid., 111.
7. G. Papásogli, *Teresa von Avila* (Paderborn, 1959), 304.
8. Letter of January 1574, cited as in Herbstrith, *Teresa von Avila*, 133.
9. Letter of July 16, 1574, cited as in Herbstrith, *Teresa von Avila*, 135.
10. Letter of December 12, 1576, cited as in Herbstrith, *Teresa von Avila*, 140.
11. Letter of March 28, 1581, cited as in Herbstrith, *Teresa von Avila*, 145.

2. THE SPIRITUAL EXPERIENCE

1. Cf. Edith Stein, "Wege der Gotteserkenntnis. Die 'Symbolische Theologie' des Areopagiten und ihre sachlichen Voraussetzungen" in *Tijdschrift voor Philosophie* (1946), 8, 1, 40.
2. Avila, *Collected Works*, 284.

3. Ibid., 288.
4. Cf. St. John of the Cross, *The Collected Works of* (Washington: ICS Publications 1979), 627-28.
5. Avila, *Collected Works*, 288.
6. Cf. Theresia von Jesu, *Leben*, 108.
7. Avila, *Collected Works*, 323.
8. Ibid., 324.
9. John of the Cross, *Collected Works*, 601.
10. Avila, *Collected Works*, 324.
11. Cf. A. Rosenberg, "Meditationsmethoden in Ost und West" in *Türen nach innen*, 97.
12. Avila, *Collected Works*, 441-442.
13. Ibid., 447.
14. Ibid., 443.
15. Ibid., 446.
16. Ibid., 444.
17. Ibid., 447.
18. Ibid., 447-448.
19. Ibid., 450.
20. Ibid., 451-452.

II. JOHN OF THE CROSS

1. SPIRITUAL DIRECTION

1. John of the Cross, *Collected Works*, 703.
2. Cf. J. Sudbrack, *Beten ist menschlich* (Freiburg i. Br., 1973), 50.
3. John of the Cross, *Collected Works*, 626.
4. A. Gerken, *Theologie der Eucharistie* (München, 1973), 66.
5. John of the Cross, *Collected Works*, 627.
6. Ibid.
7. Ibid.

2. PERSONAL MEDITATION

1. John of the Cross, *Collected Works*, 70.
2. Ibid., 636.
3. Ichiro Okumura, *Erwachen zu Gott. Ein japanischer Christ bekennt sich zum Gebet* (Bergen-Enkheim, 1976), 29.
4. Theresia von Jesu, *Leben*, 91.
5. John of the Cross, *Collected Works*, 158.
6. Ibid., 204.
7. Ibid., 289.
8. K. Hemmerle, "Christliche Spiritualität in einer pluralistischen Gesellschaft" in J. Sauger (ed.), *Glaubenserfahrung und Meditation* (Freiburg-Basel-Wien, 1975), 106.
9. John of the Cross, *Collected Works*, 156.
10. Ibid., 224.
11. John of the Cross, *Die dunkle Nacht und die Gedichte* (Einsiedeln, 1961), 99.
12. John of the Cross, *Collected Works*, 630-31.
13. John of the Cross, *Das Lied der Liebe* (Einsiedeln, 1963), 181.
14. John of the Cross, *Empor den Karmelberg* (Einsiedeln, 1964), 29.
15. John of the Cross, *Collected Works*, 141.
16. Ibid., 149.
17. Ibid.
18. John of the Cross, *Empor den Karmelberg*, 22f.
19. Ibid., 62 and 74.
20. John of the Cross, *Die lebendige Flamme, die Briefe und kleinen Schriften* (Einsiedeln, 1964), 82.
21. Ibid., 108-9.
22. John of the Cross, *Collected Works*, 113.
23. John of the Cross, *Die lebendige Flamme*, 176.
24. Ibid., 127.
25. John of the Cross, *Collected Works*, 282.
26. Ibid., 223.

27. Ibid., 114.
28. Ibid., 112-113.
29. Ibid., 103 and 104.
30. Ibid., 108.
31. Ibid., 224-25.
32. John of the Cross, *Die lebendige Flamme*, 176.
33. John of the Cross, *Empor den Karmelberg*, 25.
34. Ibid., 86 and 145.
35. Ibid., 215.
36. John of the Cross, *Collected Works*, 581.
37. Ibid., 608.
38. Ibid., 649.

III. THERESE OF LISIEUX

1. St. Thérèse of Lisieux, *Story Of A Soul* (Washington: ICS Publications, 1976), 29.
2. Ibid., 33-34.
3. Ibid., 74-75.
4. Ibid., 86.
5. Ibid., 87.
6. Ibid., 88.
7. Ibid., 102.
8. Ibid., 125.
9. Therese vom Kinde Jesus, *Selbstbiographische Schriften* (Einsiedeln, 1958), 98.
10. Ibid., 141.
11. Céline Martin, *Meine Schwester Therese* (Wien-München, 1961), 57.
12. Lisieux, *Story Of A Soul*, 242.

IV. EDITH STEIN

1. STRICKEN BY GOD

1. Edith Stein, *Aus dem Leben einer jüdischen Familie,*

Edith Steins Werke (Louvain-Freiburg i.Br., 1965), Vol. VII, 173.

2. W. Herbstrith (Teresia a Matre Dei OCD), *Das wahre Gesicht Edith Steins* (Bergen-Enkheim, 1973), 44.

3. Edith Stein, "Beiträge zur philosophischen Begründung der Psychologie und der Geisteswissenschaften: Psychische Kausalität" in *Jahrbuch für Philosophie und phänomenologische Forschung* (Halle 1922), Vol. V, 43.

4. Edith Stein, *Das Weihnachtsgeheimnis* (Selbstverlag Karmel Cologne, 1950), 13.

5. Edith Stein, *Kreuzeswissenschaft. Studie über Joannes a Cruce, Edith Steins Werke*, Vol. I, 241.

6. Kölner Selig- und Heiligsprechungsprozess (Articuli) der Dienerin Gottes Sr. Teresia Benedicta a Cruce (Edith Stein), 1962, 92.

7. Herbstrith, *Das wahre Gesicht Edith Steins*, 192.

2. SUGGESTIONS FOR MEDITATION

1. Sr. Teresia Renata de Spiritu Sancto, *Edith Stein-eine grosse Frau unseres Jahrhunderts* (Freiburg i.Br., 1962), 84.

2. Ibid., 85.

3. Ibid., 86.

THE PRAYERS OF TERESA OF AVILA

Thomas Alvarez, O.C.D. (ed.)

"Fr. Alvarez has gathered together the written prayers of St. Teresa, using many of her works. The prayers are deeply personal and introduce the reader to the school of prayer which St. Teresa taught her followers. Fr. Alvarez's commentary is often illuminating."

New Heaven/New Earth

"We have all been somewhat embarrassed by the utterances of those in love. But if the one so afflicted is a poet, as Teresa is, what you get is poetry, or perhaps music. One feels almost shy reading these words, as if one has come unannounced upon lovers. . . . Truly a classic."

New Oxford Review

Series "Profiles"   3d printing
ISBN 1-56548-065-1, paper, 136 pp.

THE PRAYERS OF JOHN OF THE CROSS

Alphonse Ruiz, O.C.D. (ed.)

"Ruiz maps out the prayer life of the great Spanish mystic and, even more important, he shows the reader precisely how to read the map. The first part comprises the saint's maxims and other short sayings and a number of dialogues and soliloquies. The second part consists of brief reflections on the nature of prayer."

B.C.Catholic

Series: "Profiles"
ISBN 0-911782-91-5, paper, 128 pp.

Also available from New City Press:

THERESE OF LISIEUX—A DISCOVERY OF LOVE
Selected Spiritual Writings
Terence Carey, O.C.D. (ed.)

"These selections from the *Story of a Soul* and the *General Correspondence* of Thérèse seek to show her to be an authentic teacher of the spiritual life."

Theology Digest

"Dividing her life into five periods, Carey illustrates her attractive personality through her own writings and letters."

Prairie Messenger

Series "Profiles"
ISBN 1-56548-014-7, paper, 144 pp.

FROM ASH TO FIRE—A Contemporary Journey
through the Interior Castle of Teresa of Avila
by Carolyn Humphreys

"After situating Teresa's work in the context of Carmelite tradition and a contemporary understanding of holistic spirituality, [Humphreys] devotes a chapter to each of the seven mansions. This is a good introduction to this important spiritual classic."

Spiritual Book News

"St. Teresa has inspired many books of commentary and I think Humphreys' book ranks with some of the best literary efforts of this era."

S. Schulein, O.C.D.S.

Series: "Spirituality"   **2d printing**
ISBN 1-56548-012-0, paper, 160 pp.

THE PRAYERS OF SAINT FRANCIS

W. Bader (ed.)

Fifty-five of St. Francis' most beautiful prayers, including "The Canticle of Creatures," "The Divine Praises," and "A Prayer for Assisi."

"After a brief introduction describing Francis' spirituality, the author gives a fresh English translation of prayers that Francis prayed, whether found in his writings properly speaking, or in the writings of Francis' biographers. . . . The book concludes with Celano's 'Portrait of Francis' and a chronological table. Highly recommended."

The Cord

Series: "Profiles"   3d printing
ISBN 1-56548-066-X, paper, 112 pp.

FROM SCRIPTURE TO LIFE

by Chiara Lubich

"*From Scripture to Life* contains commentaries that author Chiara Lubich has written on 12 different 'Words of Life' practiced by the Focolare Movement, which she founded. . . . Each section of the book includes true stories of people who applied the teaching of the Scripture passage."

Catholic News Service

"Her message is a simple one of testimony and example, of anecdotes and lessons, all based on her reading of Scripture"

B.C. Catholic

Series: "Christian Living—A Spirituality of Unity"
ISBN 0-911782-83-4, paper, 112 pp.